A Journey of

Change

The Supernatural Power of Truth

Tony Howson

DESTINY IMAGE® EUROPE
Via Maiella, 1
66020 San Giovanni Teatino (Ch) - Italy

ISBN 10: 88-89127-33-3
ISBN 13: 978 88-89127-33-9

For Worldwide Distribution. Printed in Italy.

1 2 3 4 5 6 7 8/10 09 08 07 06

This book and all other Destiny Image Europe books are available at Christian bookstores and distributors worldwide.

To order products, or for any other correspondence:

DESTINY IMAGE® EUROPE
Via Acquacorrente, 6
65123 - Pescara - Italy
Tel. +39 085 4716623 - Fax: +39 085 4716622
E-mail: info@eurodestinyimage.com

Or reach us on the Internet:
www.eurodestinyimage.com

DEDICATION

I dedicate this book to my wife and family, Margaret, Luke and Beki. Their support and patience over the years and their individual faith have been my greatest inspiration in God.

Acknowledgements

Margaret has been amazing, reading the manuscript and discussing so much with me. As this is my first book, there are so many other people I could mention. So I thank all those whose names might not appear in this paragraph. Ed and Katie Paxton figure highly as perhaps the first who challenged my comfortable theology. Here in Wrexham Nick and Sue Pengelly had (and still have) incredible patience with me going through processes as the Spirit has revolutionized my theology.

Paul Stevens, my friend and colleague who pressed me so hard to complete the manuscript.

Robin and Claire Dillamore long-standing friends who always believe in me...and tell me.

I also acknowledge posthumously the theological conversations with Bryn Jones towards the end of his life and when his own theology was undergoing Holy Spirit transformation.

Countless friends and church leaders across the UK (too many to mention by name) and Philippe and Selina in France.

Genuine friends in North America including the Godinez family in Michigan, Randy Gearhart, my good friend Gayle Brandon and a special mention of Mike and Penny Proctor who have stayed updated on the progress of the book.

Destiny Image Europe has been amazing with me in all they have done.

Finally, Gerald Coates who patiently read the whole manuscript and generously wrote the foreword. Gerald counts as a friend and a genuine source to me as another Truth seeker.

TABLE OF CONTENTS

Part Four—New Testament Writers

Part Five —The Truth of Knowledge

FOREWORD

What is the truth? The truth about Jesus, the truth about the Holy Spirit, the truth about the Church, the truth about the Kingdom, the truth about holiness and the truth about judgement, the truth about the gifts of the Holy Spirit, particularly prophecy and the truth about women in leadership and ministry.

These and more are covered in Tony Howson's publication that you have in your hands right now.

Today in certain respects there is a sort of "cloud of not knowing" around. The truth of heaven and hell is out of fashion well the truth of hell is at least. The truth about there being only one way to the Father, through Jesus Christ is not a 21st Century "who can know" post modern idea. The truth that the Christian faith is unique in so many ways and regarded by many as superior to other faiths is scoffed at in TV debates and radio shows. In my time I have taken part in sufficient Radio 2, 4 and 5 programmes and mainstream television for BBC1 and ITV to know, that when it comes to faith, and particularly the Christian faith, biblical truth is barely palatable. And often the only way presenters and commentators cope with evangelicals, is to confuse us with fundamentalists. I am not into fundamentalism; fundamentalism is no fun, mainly mental and full of isms. And the BBC has never quite worked out the difference between an evangelical and a fundamentalist just as they have never quite worked out the difference between an evangelist and an evangelical. Recently I read in a national newspaper that there were 65,000 evangelists at Spring Harvest this year. I paused and thought, "Would to God that were true"!

And yet it is impossible in most other spheres of life to function without truth. It is impossible to do history and understand the past without the concept of truth. Real people did real things in real space and time. Equally it would be just as impossible to do geography and travel across ones own country or to other nations without the concept of truth. When I buy a train ticket for Waterloo I truly believe I am going to end up in Waterloo. If the sign on the platform says that this is the Waterloo train, and the train sign says you are on the way to Waterloo, you have every right to believe it. Of course we could be on our way to Epsom Downs, but then British Rail would not be telling me the truth.

Somebody designed my car engine, and the truth is, when it goes wrong, people who know about my car engine and its design, know how to repair it. How weird it would be if my car broke down and I called the AA. The patrolman lifts the bonnet, grunts, nods, and points here and there and then says to me "well, it is true that I have experience, but I wonder what you think. I don't want to come across as superior, or that I know more than you do. I feel I need to be inclusive as I endeavour to discover what the situation is here." Then the RAC passes and he calls him in, and they discuss that it could be this, that or the other. Then some passers by, they get involved in the fray. I would be exasperated. The truth of whether I had run out of petrol, have a flat battery, or the alternator has gone would be obvious to any trained mechanic. The key to the repair is recognizing the truth of what has gone wrong and therefore this will act as a key to the truth of how it will be repaired.

Medicine takes us down an even more delicate route. Wrong diagnoses can mean wrong medication. Looking for the truth as to the results of being overweight, or drinking too much alcohol, or innocently acquiring some life threatening disease is the only way to providing longevity of life and pain control.

Foreword

So why is truth regarded as being irrelevant when it comes to creation and redemption, faith and behaviour?

It is primarily because they don't know the truth about God the Father, God the Son and God the Holy Spirit. They think God is up there, out there and distant, uninvolved in time and space. They are unaware of the truth of other powers that cannot be seen, they are evil, destructive and violent. And the truth is, we are all caught up in a battle and there are losses in battles.

Everybody wants God to be a cross between Superman and Father Christmas. But nobody wants him interfering in his or her lives. It is the other guy or the other nation or the other situation that God should intervene in.

So—truth is vital if we are going to be set free from the lies, illusions and self-opinionated perspectives that hinder us, from ever discovering why we are here.

Taking part in radio and TV programmes I have come across many atheists. It is now my firm conviction that most atheists do believe in God they just hate him. Svetlana the daughter of Stalin told the atheist turned Christian friend of mine Malcolm Muggeridge, that the last thing her father did on his deathbed was to raise his fist to God and then he breathed his last.

Now, Tony doesn't pretend to be a theologian. And you might be grateful for that. But he does use a great deal of scripture to allow biblical truth to shape our thinking, perspectives, attitudes and behaviour. And if these insights whet your appetite for something more, your local Christian bookshop or the website is the place to go to study some of these subjects in greater depth. But most of us don't start with theologians we are frightened of them.

The truth is, as A. W. Tozer has said "whatever drops into your mind when you think about God—is the most important thing about you".

Allow the truth of these pages to shatter untruth, illusion and fantasy, build truth into your thinking, responding, speaking and usefulness.

Gerald Coates
Speaker, author, broadcaster and pioneer.

INTRODUCTION

"The whole Truth and nothing but the Truth."

That's what this book is about—how we find out what is Truth. We need to know Truth because when we know it, it sets us free. Consider the following passage from the Book of John:

> Some of the multitudes therefore, when they heard these words, were saying, "This certainly is the Prophet." Others were saying, "This is the Christ." Still others were saying, "Surely the Christ is not going to come from Galilee, is He?" Has not the Scripture said that the Christ comes from the offspring of David, and from Bethlehem, the village where David was? So there arose a division in the multitude because of Him. And some of them wanted to seize Him, but no one laid hands on Him. The officers therefore came to the chief priests and Pharisees, and they said to them, "Why did you not bring Him?" The officers answered, "Never did a man speak the way this man speaks." The Pharisees therefore answered them, "You have not also been led astray, have you? No one of the rulers or Pharisees has believed in Him, has he? But this multitude which does not know the Law is accursed." Nicodemus

said to them (he who came to Him before, being one of them), "Our Law does not judge a man, unless it first hears from him and knows what he is doing, does it?" They answered and said to him, "You are not also from Galilee, are you? Search, and see that no prophet arises out of Galilee." And everyone went to his home (John 7:40-53).

This is only one of the occasions when Jesus caused division over who He was and who He claimed to be.

We can, and need to, learn from what John shared with us in this passage. The dispute was a typical confrontation between Spirit and "theology." There is a true theology, which comes by the Spirit. There is another that speaks from intellect. All that Jesus taught was by the Spirit. Every word He uttered came from the Father—all by revelation.

Scripture makes it clear that we realize who Jesus is by revelation. In this passage dispute erupted because Jesus was moving in the supernatural. This was not only concerning His deeds; it was also because of His teaching (*"Never did a man speak the way this man speaks"*). However, the issue was argued on what they knew and from a predetermined position. So we can note the following:

❖ They argued that the Messiah did not come from Galilee.

❖ He should be born in and come from Bethlehem.

❖ Those who followed Jesus were Galileans.

❖ They were all taken in by Jesus' teaching.

They spoke judgments *on the basis of what they did not know*. I wonder how many of us, have done that? They all spoke from a safe position; it was all reasoned argument—but it had nothing to do with the Spirit. Our understanding of God comes essentially by the Spirit. The people referred to in the passage were mistaken because they argued from what they knew and were unwilling to change.

Jesus made it clear that Truth had to come by revelation when He said: *"It is written in the prophets, 'AND THEY SHALL ALL BE TAUGHT OF GOD.' Everyone who has heard and learned from the Father, comes to Me"* (John 6:45).

Introduction

If *theology* is the study of God, then it seems to me that such theology should be experiential in the first place. From the beginning of time, it has been clear that people came to understand God because they encountered Him.

That was not only true then; it is also essential to today's study of God. I know so many people whose experience of God has changed them. It has done more than that. Their experience has also changed their thinking and lifestyle. Our doctrine and the way we live go hand in hand. Wrong teaching produces a wrong way of living. That is why many students of the Bible and countless controversial movements based on the Bible have gone astray into a way of living, which is clearly unacceptable before God.

This book is about the experience of the Truth of God. It does not plunge into the depths of understanding or theological controversy. It is my hope and intention for it to be an effective handbook for all those who remain seekers after the Truth. The Scriptures tell us that human wisdom alone does not take us into the knowledge and presence of God. It is to the have-nots God reveals Himself.

Be open to the Spirit as you read this book. And when you've completed the reading, please keep seeking after the Truth by the Spirit.

Part One

DISCOVERING THE TRUTH

Chapter One

EXPERIENCE THE TRUTH

I was in my late teens, regularly attending church and singing in the choir both services every Sunday—as though I was doing God and the people a favor. Because my family moved frequently (because of my father's work) I attended several different schools. Toward the end of my school career, we moved back to a familiar area and I went to see a former school friend. I found out that his father managed a Christian conference center and I attended services with him—after all, I *was* a Christian.

My friend invited me back the following Sunday for a youth meeting held in a barn. I arrived an hour early and listened to my friend's father speak about the Cross. In my intellect I found it interesting. Later, at the youth service, they showed a very old movie about Christian young people travelling in the Philippines who played basketball and shared the Gospel with young people there. The crux of the film was the moment when the leader of the team talked with one of the young men, showing him in Romans 12:1 the need to present ourselves as living sacrifices to God.

I was suddenly presented with the hypocrisy of my own selfish life, how in my arrogance I was doing God and His people a favor. I was devastated. I drove home with tears pouring down my face. I went straight to bed, knowing that my face would betray my tears. I knelt by my bed and prayed for the first time in years: *God my life isn't good enough. You come and take over.* I meant it. God heard it. He came into my life and changed me. I had been on tranquillizers and suddenly no longer needed them. I couldn't say I was converted, born again, or anything else; all I knew was that I was different on the inside.

It was not on the basis of my *understanding* but rather my *experience* that I came to the Truth. Conversion is beyond comprehension—just like the peace it brings. The Truth reached me because of the work of the Spirit of Truth. It's all to do with the Holy Spirit. He is the source of Absolute Truth. It's only through the Holy Spirit we can really know and experience God. Since God is Truth, we need to know Him if we are to know the Truth. Perhaps you can relate to some of my story?

As I sit here writing this after over 30 years of church leadership, I have to admit that my new birth was not my first experience of God. I was about 14 years old when my mother made three stipulations. One was that I should not become a church minister or a policeman. My mother was wise—at least in human terms. The reason for her stipulations: I was the son of a policeman and she had noticed how isolated children could become because of their parents' occupation.

About that same time, our church minister asked me to read for him at meetings—which I did every Sunday. He had me rehearse them so I could get used to speaking to a congregation without a public address system. One evening after my rehearsal the minister said, "Have you ever thought of going into the ministry"? I mumbled something like "not really," but felt deeply convicted inside. I knew God wanted me to do exactly that—become a church minister.

Well, I went home and said to my mother, "What would you say if I told you I was thinking of becoming a church minister"? Her reply was immediate: "You'll do no such thing…" and she went on for quite a long time telling me why! In spite of all her words, from that day forward, I knew God decided my long-term destiny. When I later began my teaching career, I knew it was not to be my long-term career. I had experienced God.

I had felt the convicting presence and power of the Holy Spirit. Again, I didn't know the language but there was no questioning the experience!

Do you identify with my situation and experience so far? From here they become more controversial. The ongoing realization of Truth in me and to me has always been by the Spirit—it has not always been because of the Word. It's the Spirit who brings the Word to life in us.

HOLY SPIRIT BAPTISM

I had my theology in place. I could easily argue my case on baptism, the second coming, and lot of other things! The woman who later became my wife, Margaret, was a member of the same church I attended. She went on a mission trip one summer to Cornwall, England, and she returned having been baptized in the Spirit. Our church minister and his wife helped me undermine Marg's experience. His wife was quite a theologian and I was excellent at arguing my case. Within a short time Marg lost a great portion of her fire in the Spirit but never denied her experience…and I could not deny that she was different—for the better. Some time later we got married in spite of the theological difference. God told her we were to marry.

We attended a weekly Bible study and the minister told me he was going to talk about *tongues* as part of a series on the Holy Spirit. Marg and I laughed together as we discussed what his approach would be and why we thought speaking in tongues was wrong. As we sat through that evening session I could hardly believe what was happening. I heard the minister make frequent references to tongues and it was a serious study with plenty of Bible references. With every Scripture he quoted, the Holy Spirit revealed to me the reverse interpretation of what the church leader was bringing. Remember, too, that I had my own fixed view of how to interpret these passages; but with every verse, I was challenged within. My natural inclination was not to accept tongues or the Baptism in the Spirit as a "second blessing" from God. I believed I had received all I needed at the point of my conversion. What was going on was stunning and life changing. The Spirit rather than the Word was accomplishing the work.

From that evening I set out on a journey to reach the goal of God in the things of the Spirit. Some weeks later my wife heard me speaking in tongues while we were decorating a bedroom. The process began.

God had revealed Truth to me by the Spirit. My adherence to the Word had actually been a hindrance until the Spirit brought me understanding.

Perhaps we can relate this to the New Testament. We find a eunuch in the Book of Acts unable to understand what he is reading in the Scripture. The apostles' understanding of the Scriptures was also broken by what the Spirit did—their doctrine was altered. We shall look at this aspect in greater detail later. For the moment we can establish the principle that the Holy Spirit, in guiding us into all Truth, causes change to take place in and around us.

THE SPIRIT OF TRUTH

One of our problems is letting ourselves trust the Holy Spirit when we don't understand, or when we even feel we don't want to do what God is telling us to do. I'm sure you know what I mean! Notice how the New Testament expresses this dilemma:

> *We speak God's wisdom in a mystery, the hidden wisdom, which God predestined before the ages to our glory; the wisdom which none of the rulers of this age has understood; for if they had understood it, they would not have crucified the Lord of glory; but just as it is written, "THINGS WHICH EYE HAS NOT SEEN AND EAR HAS NOT HEARD, AND which HAVE NOT ENTERED THE HEART OF MAN, ALL THAT GOD HAS PREPARED FOR THOSE WHO LOVE HIM." For to us God revealed them through the Spirit; for the Spirit searches all things, even the depths of God. For who among men knows the thoughts of a man except the spirit of the man, which is in him? Even so the thoughts of God no one knows except the Spirit of God* (1 Corinthians 2:7-11).

So, the Spirit reveals what is beyond natural understanding. What our human minds cannot grasp comes to us by revelation through the Holy Spirit. That's how we come to the Truth in the first place.

It's interesting to note that on two occasions Jesus actually referred to the Spirit as the *Spirit of Truth:*

If you love Me, you will keep My commandments. And I will ask the Father, and He will give you another Helper, that He may be with you forever; that is the Spirit of truth, whom the world cannot receive, because it does not behold Him or know Him, but you know Him because He abides with you, and will be in you (John 14:15-17).

When the Helper comes, whom I will send to you from the Father, that is the Spirit of truth, who proceeds from the Father, He will bear witness of Me, and you will bear witness also, because you have been with Me from the beginning (John 15:26-27).

We will look at these thoughts in greater detail later in the book. For the moment, let's just leave it at this—the Holy Spirit is the Spirit of Truth. That means He is crucial in helping us both individually and together to come into more of the Truth. He is the One who inspired all the Scriptures. He now constantly takes us forward in Truth because He is The Spirit of Truth. It is His nature; He cannot tell a lie!

TESTIMONY

True testimony is by the Spirit. I'll share later that it is possible to say things that are true and yet not be speaking the Truth. Motives, for example, can be wrong.

The word *testimony* is found several times in the New Testament. It comes from the Greek word for "a witness," and from this word comes the English word "martyr." Testimony has to do with speaking the truth. However this truth comes from within the person. It is not the knowledge of history or passages of literature. It is Truth spoken from within and it expresses our experience of God by the Spirit.

Let's look at the New Testament to get some good understanding.

Testimony has to do with "cost." That's why "martyr" in English comes from the Greek word for "testimony." Stephen's testimony cost him his life (see Acts 6:10-13; 7:52-60) and speaks of personal experience. Our experience influences our destiny. Our experience of the Holy Spirit takes us into further revelations of the Truth. It was true of all those who were significant in Old Testament times. It was also true at the time when the New Testament was being lived, particularly in the disciples of Jesus.

So, as we take a look at ourselves, we too should be living in the days of the Spirit. These are still Holy Spirit days because He is still with us. It's a place in the Spirit where our own experience of God, the supernatural realm and everyday life, causes us to grow and learn by experience and revelation. This excitement must return to the Church of God. It will not be achieved by more of the same unbelief. We have to change and become men and women of the Spirit, not just live through what we have heard others say. There is a real Word basis for this experience. Apostle Paul wrote: "...*I will go on to visions and revelations of the Lord*" (2 Cor. 12:1).

We will spend some time later looking at the life of Paul. For the moment, let's consider that the man who wrote this verse was a first-class teacher and theologian. He, with all his knowledge and experience of life, wanted to move forward in visions and revelations. Why? Because he knew there was more to experience. I think we should all be of the same mind. I hope you agree.

Perhaps we can come to a place of godly dissatisfaction where we say with Paul: *I will go on...*

STEPHEN

Stephen was a man who determined to go on in spite of what he was facing from all who opposed him. He had been chosen as a man *full of the Spirit* (see Acts 6). His death was a sad day for the church in many ways: yet it also brought blessing. We can learn from his life. No matter how difficult situations may become, God remains good and is constantly at work in every area of life and each circumstance. He rules for us so even that which appears to be bad He brings about for our good. In this sense, the devil is no more than a tool in the hands of the living God. He only exists so we may know victory.

At the death of Stephen, it is interesting to note the following:

❖ Saul of Tarsus, later to become that great apostle Paul, was in agreement with the martyrdom of Stephen, but was pricked in his conscience and ultimately responded to the Lordship of Jesus. The rest of his life was given to the will of God and much of the Mediterranean area was reached with the Gospel through him. Paul's life was far from easy, but Stephen may have been an example for him. The testimony of Stephen spoke to others; our testimonies will speak to others as well.

❖ The church in Jerusalem fell under heavy persecution, but as it was scattered, so the Gospel was spread to the surrounding areas. Revival came to Samaria through Philip (see Acts 8).

EXPERIENCE

Perhaps we don't like it but experience affects us all. Every one of us has had good and bad things happen when we were younger; some of experiences were devastating, others brought genuine transformation to our lives for the better.

God made us unique. We each have a special awareness of time and history as we progress through life. Everyone has a beginning and an end, and much goes on in between! Our experiences allow us to become what we are destined for.

God created us. He knows us and helps us change for the better so we can be more useful in society and life in general. God is for us and wants the best for us in everything. His Word makes this desire clear: "...I [Jesus] *came that they may have life, and have it abundantly*" (John 10:10). And *"We are disciplined by the Lord in order that we may not be condemned along with the world"* (1 Cor. 11:32).

Discipline is a harsh concept in the 21st century. It is unpopular because it has a negative feel to it. This is because most people who bring discipline to us have failed to bring with it the essential ingredient—love. God loves us. His discipline allows us to avoid condemnation, avoid living under the black cloud called guilt. His discipline sets us free from our past mistakes. He then re-establishes us on our way.

And we know that God causes all things to work together for good to those who love God, to those who are called according to His purpose (Romans 8:28).

God uses our experiences of life. He also interrupts our daily living when He needs to. In this way, He guides us through life by His Spirit: Romans 8:28 contains a principle we need to recognize and in every circumstance: Faith recognizes the goodness of God when things in life are not going well just as much as when everything seems fine.

> *For all who are being led by the Spirit of God, these are sons of God* (Romans 8:14).

These are some of the means by which God works to establish what He calls *truth in the innermost being* (see Psalm 51:6). It is on this understanding, inward truth being established by experience, that this book is written. True theology is experience of God and not the knowledge of facts.

I live and write from my experiences with God. He works in each us individually...

MEETING GOD

Almost everyone at some time has decided to discover God. Some people have tried reading the Bible, others pray, some fast. Others have used the same things you have and succeeded in finding the Lord. Others have failed. So what is the difference? It has to do with the attitude with which we seek Him:

> *But from there you will seek the LORD your God, and you will find Him if you search for Him with all your heart and all your soul* (Deuteronomy 4:29).

Discovering God requires total commitment. However, God promises that if we do seek Him then we shall find Him. He actually wants us to meet Him and He tells us how: *"And without faith it is impossible to please Him, for he who comes to God must believe that He is, and that He is a rewarder of those who seek Him"* (Heb. 11:6).

Any difficulty in this process can be overcome. Why? God will equip and empower us because He is on our side.

The key is unhesitating faith because:

❖ We come to Him by faith.

❖ We believe that He exists.

❖ We seek Him.

❖ We seek Him with all our hearts.

You see the Truth of God comes to us by revelation. Revelation is experience. No matter how much we read the Bible, meditate, pray, sacrifice, or anything else, God will only make Himself known to us by revelation. Many people have died disillusioned because they never *found* God. One man I knew years ago had read the Bible from cover to cover three times and yet took his own life. He did not apply faith as he read. The Bible alone brings the truth *about* God but it does not, on its own, bring the truth *from* God. That only comes by the Spirit of Truth as He reveals that Truth to us.

Chapter Two

TRUTH IS NOT THE TRUTH

I've heard it said "there are lies, damned lies, and statistics." It's true. You may have noticed how two politicians of opposing parties can totally contradict each other because they quote different statistics. It can be so confusing. However, a statistic that is true may not reveal the (full) truth because it only expresses one angle of a situation.

Likewise, people can use the same words but mean different things by what we say or how we say or write them. An individual conviction about something, strongly expressed, doesn't mean a person is telling the truth. Discussing specific ways of thinking produces debate. No one knows everything, but we like to think we do. At least, that's how we speak sometimes!

I suppose we've all talked with people who don't tell us the whole truth. They just convey the part of the truth they want us to know. They hide everything else and give us a wrong impression. King Saul was like that. He told the prophet Samuel part of the truth but pretended it was all the truth; it wasn't. Saul exemplifies people who tell us things and although what they said may be true, the problem is they haven't told us the whole truth. We are left with a wrong impression. In the end we believe a lie, but we assume it's the truth. This may cause us to become judgmental toward another person who is, in fact, innocent concerning what has been said. We may take an enemy's position toward someone who might be blameless and in need of our friendship.

Jesus made it clear that when you know the truth, the truth sets you free (see John 8:32). Unfortunately, when you only know *part* of the truth, you are not even partly set free. You are actually in bondage and confusion. If you know someone is in the habit of telling you only parts of the truth, then you cannot trust what is said. In fact, you don't trust the person and can't confide in them. The way a person speaks tells you what they're like. If they talk to you about someone else behind their back, you can also assume they're doing the same about you too!

So partial truth is, in fact, a lie.

Why is this true? It has to do with motive. Truth is only truth when it is expressed from a pure heart. David wrote about truth in the *"inward parts"* (Ps. 51:6). When anyone speaks from a wrong motive, it is not the truth. It generally reveals something wrong at the person's heart level. Notice the clear way this idea is expressed in the New Testament:

> But the Spirit explicitly says that in later times some will fall away from the faith, paying attention to deceitful spirits and doctrines of demons, by means of the hypocrisy of liars seared in their own conscience as with a branding iron, men who forbid marriage and advocate abstaining from foods, which God has created to be gratefully shared in by those who believe and know the truth. For everything created by God is good, and nothing is to be rejected, if it is received with gratitude; for it is sanctified by means of the word of God and prayer (1 Timothy 4:1-5).

This passage that Paul wrote to Timothy speaks of depth. Watch the process that takes place:

❖ There is demonic invasion. It brings deceit—in other words, there is a removal of part of the Truth. That's what deceit is. It results in wrong doctrine.

❖ Deceit leads to hypocrisy, lies, and a removal of conscience.

❖ Finally, legalism sets in with the introduction of repressive rules and regulations.

This process took place with Adam and Eve. Their life began in conditions where nothing was hidden because there was nothing to hide! They were innocent. Demonic invasion came through the serpent. He asked questions; he undermined:

> Now the serpent was more crafty than any beast of the field which the LORD God had made. And he said to the woman, "Indeed, has God said, 'You shall not eat from any tree of the garden'?" And the woman said to the serpent, "From the fruit of the trees of the garden we may eat; but from the fruit of the tree which is in the middle of the garden, God has said, 'You shall not eat from it or touch it, lest you die.'" And the serpent said to the woman, "You surely shall not die"! (Genesis 3:1-4)

One question leads to another until the serpent states: *you surely shall not die!* He undermines what God said. He doesn't actually call God a liar: he just implies it and undermines trust and faith. This is deception. It is totally opposed to the Truth from God. We recognize this fact because of what happened to Adam and Eve. Suddenly, having eaten the fruit, their sin is uncovered (since they are naked). They feel the need to cover themselves. Deception has stolen their liberty.

This is what Paul speaks of in First Timothy 4. He points out that deceiving spirits will influence the Church and oppose the Truth God brings to His people by the Spirit. There is a lack of gratitude and basic relationship with God, a failure in Word and prayer.

So, only part of the truth is not God's Truth. In fact, when only some of the truth is told, it is deliberate deceit. It is the devil that deceives. True doctrine and righteous living go hand in hand. Where life is lived in hypocrisy, then it follows that the teaching is wrong, even if it is intellectually accurate. So let's see how this is represented in the Gospels.

JESUS

In Matthew 15, Jesus has a conversation with some of the Pharisees. He challenges them about their adherence to tradition rather than the commandment of God. In this context, as with Paul, Jesus points to the hypocrisy of these people. He says:

> *"You hypocrites, rightly did Isaiah prophesy of you, saying, 'THIS PEO-*
> *PLE HONORS ME WITH THEIR LIPS, BUT THEIR HEART IS*
> *FAR AWAY FROM ME. BUT IN VAIN DO THEY WORSHIP*
> *ME, TEACHING AS DOCTRINES THE PRECEPTS OF MEN'"*
> (Matthew 15:7-9).

I think it's fair to say they were hypocrites. Why? First of all, Jesus said so! They were teaching from a human perspective. They were talking as from God but what they said was not from Him. They gave a false impression about God and totally misrepresented Him. In the context of this passage that was even happening in their worship! Their words were not from pure hearts. That's why Jesus quoted to them *"their heart is far from"* me. Jesus said that true worshipers worship in Spirit and *truth* (see John 4:24). We don't have a choice. We must have both Spirit *and* truth. So hypocrisy has no place in the worship of God. The fruit of such actions is displeasing to Him. That is why we need to have the Spirit. He guides us *into* all the Truth. With the Holy Spirit, Truth is inner, not just what is expressed on the outside.

Satan traps us in legalism. You can be in the worship service praising God yet be totally bound because satan is reminding you of things you've done. God looks at the heart and asks: *Do you love me?* We know the answer is *yes.* It's good to realize that in such a case as this, the act of worship is not hypocrisy because the heart (the seat of Truth) is good. Not one of us is perfect; Thomas wasn't when he worshiped Jesus (see John 20:28). Nor was the prostitute in the house of the Pharisee (see Luke 7:36-39). Yet, on occasion, although we have done less significant things, we feel unqualified because of the accusations of the devil. We *feel* we are not worthy to worship Him, so we don't. That's what deception does to us. When we love God, it's hypocrisy *not* to worship Him!

Later in the same Matthew 15 passage Jesus says more to help His disciples understand His teaching. It also helps us today:

> *Do you not understand that everything that goes into the mouth passes into the*
> *stomach, and is eliminated? But the things that proceed out of the mouth come*

from the heart, and those defile the man. For out of the heart come evil thoughts, murders, adulteries, fornications, thefts, false witness, slanders. These are the things, which defile the man; but to eat with unwashed hands does not defile the man (Matthew 15:17:20).

So defilement comes from inside the individual. Before God, it's the inner person that is all-important. The human spirit, or the heart, is the seat of personal truth.

Many people today would be offended if Jesus spoke about them in the way He spoke to the Pharisees! That's probably true about a lot of what He said. The sad thing is not that such rebuke was needed but the fact that it could be said about so many believers! Perhaps this remains true today. I wonder how many people would walk away from a local church because they were told the Truth by the church leader or a visiting ministry. Even as believers, we may not like the Truth when God delivers it to us. However, when the Truth does come to us, our response says a great deal about us.

Jesus wrote seven individual letters to seven churches in the Book of Revelation. To most of the churches He had strong things to say. However, for each church there was room for repentance. More than that, there was opportunity for every individual within those churches to become free. That's why for each church, Jesus writes: *to him who. . .* which explains division within the church. Some don't like the Truth; others accept it. Unity and division have to do with Spirit, not doctrine. That's why people who agree on so much head knowledge can disagree and separate when it comes to agreeing about Spiritual things. The wrestling for Truth takes place in the heart, not the head! Lack of repentance reveals what is in the heart.

Are we ready to repent when that's what we need to do—regardless of position? I believe we must. That's how the Truth is safeguarded; that Truth is part of us, not just in our understanding. When, as believers, we repent we enthrone again the righteousness of God in us. We release ourselves from bondage and allow the Truth to set us free again. The results are dramatic!

"Oh," you say, "I'm born again. I'm filled with the Spirit." I thank God you are! But I also think there are things in Scripture we all need to understand. Peter was an apostle of Jesus. He lived under His direct leadership. Yet Jesus at one point addressed Peter as satan! Let's look at the context:

*From that time Jesus Christ began to show His disciples that He must go to
Jerusalem, and suffer many things from the elders and chief priests and scribes,
and be killed, and be raised up on the third day. And Peter took Him aside and
began to rebuke Him, saying, "God forbid it, Lord! This shall never happen to
You." But He turned and said to Peter, "Get behind Me, Satan! You are a
stumbling block to Me; for you are not setting your mind on God's interests, but
man's"* (Matthew 16:21-23).

This is strong stuff! Peter meant well. He didn't want Jesus to suffer. He
tried to help. He wanted to encourage Jesus. Unfortunately what seemed
to be nice, thoughtful words were actually inspired by the devil! Having
good intentions or saying nice things does not mean that our words are
the truth. The enemy can even inspire them! Sentiment can be dangerous. How many believers, I wonder, have been hindered by people saying
nice things, even suggesting that suffering is not the will of God? After all,
that is the real context of Peter's words in the passage. We need to learn
what the Spirit is saying and speak it out with love—not with sentimental-
ity. In this way we encourage and provoke faith. That's how the Word of
God works in us and how it should be working *out* of us.

The Holy Spirit doesn't always say nice things! He tells the Truth—with
love—but provoking us to an activated faith. Unfortunately we take the
short cut; we settle for saying "nice" things every time. Perhaps we can
learn this lesson now and pass it on to future generations. I believe God
wants us to raise up a final generation that won't have to keep reliving the
same mistakes because we, instead of giving the impression that we are so
perfect, actually lose all hypocrisy and tell the Truth without needing to
protect ourselves. That's living the Truth!

CHURCH LEADERSHIP

I believe that we church leaders can listen, advise, and guide believers
and still have our minds on our own interests, not the will of God. For
example, someone from the local church (usually a young person who
hasn't learned how things are *controlled* in church yet) approaches a
leader because they feel God has spoken to them. The leader listens care-
fully, and then says, *"Go away and pray about it."* It sounds so spiritual, but
frequently it's a cop-out. This advice has nothing to do with the words of

Jesus or what the human authors of the Bible wrote. How *dare* we use the concept of prayer to control and manipulate people.

It's a shame when church leaders get caught up in the local scene and their own priorities and fail to be aware of all that God is doing in His Church. We need to obtain Heaven's perspective. We must catch the voice of the Spirit and guide those in our care. It's dangerous if we don't. A church leader brings an entire congregation of the people of God into bondage when he operates from his own agenda.

Time and space prohibits me from delving further into this topic—perhaps I'll write another book! Suffice it to say, church leaders are the role models. Our hearts either convey the Truth of God or we act in hypocrisy. If we don't get it right, the church is bound by us and people will leave.

Satan and the demons

Don't ever forget—satan is a deceiver. He is the same deceiver today that he was in Bible days! He can still quote Scripture, just as he did when he tempted Jesus. If the devil can be bold with Jesus, he can be so with us too! Have you noticed in the Gospels how the demons knew who Jesus was?

> *And there was a man in the synagogue possessed by the spirit of an unclean demon, and he cried out with a loud voice, "Ha! What do we have to do with You, Jesus of Nazareth? Have You come to destroy us? I know who You are— the Holy One of God!" And Jesus rebuked him, saying, "Be quiet and come out of him!" And when the demon had thrown him down in their midst, he came out of him without doing him any harm. And amazement came upon them all, and they began discussing with one another saying, "What is this message? For with authority and power He commands the unclean spirits, and they come out." (Luke 4:33-36).*

Jesus was (and is) the Holy One of God. What the demon said was true—but it was not the Truth. It came from an evil heart, and was wrongly motivated. Because the source was demonic it would inspire fear, suspicion, and alienation, rather than love and trust. Do you see the importance of inner truth and pure motives? In this passage, Jesus actually cast out a demon that spoke things that were true because the motive (the source) was evil. It's only by the Spirit of Truth that we can see beyond the words. This is achieved by operating in what the New Testament calls *the gift of discerning (or distinguishing) of Spirits* (see 1 Cor. 12:10). To some extent we can all, in any case, recognize the flesh or demonic activity because we are spiritual (see 1 Cor. 2:14,15).

If faith, love, integrity, and trust are not present in the one who speaks, then it is not the truth coming from God. It just doesn't ring true in the heart of the hearer who is in touch with the Spirit of God. Partial truth and wrong motivation produce lies, not the truth. Inner truth is the only truth that matters. In the words of Jesus: *"the mouth speaks out of that which fills the heart"* (Matt. 12:34).

Some facts about demons:

❖ Demons can say things that may be true but the purpose is evil, not good. They do not convey the Truth.

❖ Demons can become attached to people, going with them wherever they go. The word often used in the Bible is "possessed" which really means demonized. So individuals can become demonized, a permanent state, unless the demon is cast out.

Although Peter was not demonized, satan could put into his mouth words that seemed rightly motivated. This was a temporary experience when demonic influence and human sentiment replaced divine wisdom. This can happen to any of us as well.

If "temporary demonization" can happen to Peter, a disciple of Jesus, it can occur with anyone, even a church leader. Have you ever heard a preacher, who, in everything he says, is right, but it just feels as though what he is saying is empty, or we're not connecting with him? Discernment plays a role in how messages in the Spirit are received. Although we should not expect perfection from a church leader or preacher, equally, everyone who carries responsibility in the Church of God should guard himself from falling into the trap that caught Peter. Teaching and sharing the Word of God needs to come by the Spirit; it should be in life; the heart of the speaker must be genuine.

In the New Testament the Pharisees are a clear example of hypocritical teaching. They assumed that they were the children of Abraham; and frankly this is understandable. Physically speaking Abraham was the Father of the nation. All of Israel (with some notable exceptions of people who changed nationality like Ruth) was a direct descendant from Abraham. He was their father; and according to Scripture they had the right to claim this. Jesus had strong words to say to them in response to their assumptions:

> They answered and said to Him, "Abraham is our father." Jesus said to them, "If you are Abraham's children, do the deeds of Abraham. But as it is, you are seeking to kill me, a man who has told you the truth, which I heard from God; this Abraham did not do. You are doing the deeds of your father." They said to Him, "We were not born of fornication; we have one Father, even God" (John 8:39-41).

Jesus does not question the natural descent from Abraham. His response here places Him in a spiritual relationship with Abraham. Jesus' claim is that He hears from the Father. They then lay the same claim both for Abraham and themselves. In doing this they call into being a *spiritual* source of life for themselves as well as for Jesus. Jesus' reply appears to be judgmental. He is scathing with these religious but unreal people.

> [Jesus said] "You are of your father the devil, and you want to do the desires of your father. He was a murderer from the beginning, and does not stand in the truth, because there is no truth in him. Whenever he speaks a lie, he speaks from his own nature; for he is a liar, and the father of lies" (John 8:44).

This statement clarifies the basis on which Jesus is speaking—spiritual relationship. So anyone who claims fatherhood in Abraham should do so on the same basis. This is also revealed in several passages in the New Testament Epistles.

The Pharisees were well versed in the Old Testament Scriptures. They taught the people from them. They could quote them, and in some ways they had a good understanding of them. The words they spoke were true. The great problem was the source of their words—their own hearts.

If the devil was their father, then he was the heart source of what they said. Not Abraham. How could this be if they were teachers of the Law? We would think it was impossible. It is not. In the Book of Matthew, Jesus addresses His disciples and suggests to them that they may be sheep in the *midst of wolves* (see Matt. 10:15-17). It can happen! Every leader should be on guard and have others watching over his life with him. So much pain for so many could be avoided if more would do this.

Challenges

About 70 years ago, a man of significant international ministry was presenting special meetings in a city. He was travelling with his team and visiting the United Kingdom. A woman in one of the churches in that city went to see her pastor. She said that God had shown her that the famous minister was in an adulterous relationship with his secretary who was travelling with him. She also said that he would leave the Swan Hotel where the secretary was staying at 9:30 that evening. The pastor accompanied the lady to the hotel and they waited outside the rear door. At precisely 9:30 the man came out through the door. The pastor confronted him and immediately the man of great anointing and international fame fell to his knees thanking God. He had been praying that God would get him out of the bondage he had succumbed to. No word of the affair hit the news or tabloid headlines—it was dealt with correctly behind the scenes. It is not good for man or woman to be alone! We all need to hear the Spirit voice through others. Both the Truth and the Church are then protected.

May I suggest that evil has infiltrated the Church of God because of false teaching and leadership? The issue is not whether they used the Bible in their teaching. It is again a question of *heart source*. No matter what he says or how well he says it, an unbeliever will always produce unbelief. The seed is from the heart. His heart talks to the heart of the listener. Anyone who lives under this kind of teaching will be influenced by it. It will become part of his truth even though it is false because he has been deceived. All teaching produces fruit—good or bad. It's the fruit that gives evidence of the teaching!

When Jesus heard what Peter said, He challenged him. Unfortunately, church leadership, teaching, and leadership lifestyle, have gone unchallenged. No one believes they have the right to do what Jesus saw as necessary. We do have the responsibility to bring challenge to those who may be slipping in their walk with God—whoever they may be.

We may feel challenges are no longer required. However, apostles in the New Testament still needed correction. The graphic example is, again, Peter. As an apostle he received the revelation that the Gospel was not just for the Jews. He also was the first to preach to Gentiles and see them respond to the Gospel while he was still speaking. The same Peter went to Antioch some time later and was challenged by Paul (probably considered a lesser apostle than Peter) because he ate separately with the Jews instead of eating together with the Gentiles. The irony is that Peter is the apostle who originally received from God the vision and revelation that the Gospel was for the Gentiles as well as the Jews (see Galatians 2:11-13; Acts 10:9-18).

What would have happened if Paul had not challenged Peter? The church would most likely have turned back to two separate communities with the Jews existing exclusively and apart from all foreigners. It would have been a lie. There would have been practical and theological separation of the churches with Paul and those with Peter. The challenge produced unity. It did not bring destruction and separation. If we seek the unity of which God approves, then we must be ready to challenge others...and be challenged ourselves!

So, can we face the challenge? Do we have the faith to discover the unity of the faith by standing for what is right before God and opposing what is wrong? Over the years I have been known as somewhat of a rebel when challenging the status quo. Perhaps I didn't always handle myself as well as possible; perhaps I lacked wisdom. Whatever the true situation, God has always known my heart. The question for me is whether I am still ready to pursue the practice of truth to discover even more of The Truth.

Can we believe God for a generation to rise up where the youngest can challenge some of our most accepted assumptions about what we do and why? I recall a 12-year-old girl rightly challenging me about a comment I made to her. I was glad she did it. I am still glad of it today.

It's time to let the young and old alike open their mouths and confront the ungodliness in all of us. As long as they speak from the Holy Spirit in their heart, they can help us enter further into the Truth.

Part Two

JESUS AND TRUTH

Chapter Three

EXPERIENCE WITH JESUS

The Holy Spirit on earth brings the Truth to us. He inspired the Scriptures we read. He is the source of Heaven's revelation in those writings. The eunuch written about in Acts 8 was reading from the prophecy of Isaiah. Although he was reading, he didn't understand; what's more, he knew he didn't understand! Only the Holy Spirit brings understanding.

On this subject it's worth reminding us that on two occasions Jesus referred to the Spirit as the *Spirit of Truth:*

If you love Me, you will keep My commandments. And I will ask the Father, and He will give you another Helper, that He may be with you forever; that is the Spirit of truth, whom the world cannot receive, because it does not behold Him or know Him, but you know Him because He abides with you, and will be in you (John 14:15-17).

When the Helper comes, whom I will send to you from the Father, that is the Spirit of truth, who proceeds from the Father, He will bear witness of Me, and you will bear witness also, because you have been with Me from the be-ginning (John 15:26-27).

The Book of Acts is crucial to our understanding about how God brings His Truth to His people. It is also helpful to spend time looking at Jesus' teaching because Acts is really a continuation of what God was doing through Jesus during His earthly life. As with Jesus, so we find the apostles bringing Truth by revelation of the Spirit. Since the Book of Acts helps us understand the importance of Holy Spirit revelation, this part of the Bible is a backcloth to Pentecost.

The disciples (apostles) spent three special years with Jesus. They heard His teaching; they saw what He did; they did some of it themselves. Above all, they had spent time with Him. It was true discipleship.

INTIMACY

The idea of discipleship has nothing to do with intellectual aware-ness. Head knowledge was not what Jesus brought to the twelve. The Word was in Him; it became flesh in Him. One religious group that has its own translation of the Bible takes the Greek word for the word "know" in certain passages and replaces it with the phrase *take knowledge of Him* or *have knowledge of Him* when referring to Jesus. This is not how things were. One of Jesus' twelve apostles, when writing to believers, speaks of intimacy with Jesus. The following is taken from the beginning of John's first epistle:

> *What was from the beginning, what we have heard, what we have seen with our eyes, what we beheld and our hands handled, concerning the Word of Life—and the life was manifested, and we have seen and bear witness and pro-claim to you the eternal life, which was with the Father and was manifested to us—what we have seen and heard we proclaim to you also, that you also may have fellowship with us; and indeed our fellowship is with the Father, and with His Son Jesus Christ.*

More about this passage follows later in the book, but for now it is ob-vious that John's relationship with Jesus was real and intimate, and this was what John was communicating to his audience.

Some of the things Jesus explained to the twelve were for their own ears only. There were things He did not say or explain to the crowds that followed Him. For example:

> At that time Jesus answered and said, "I praise Thee, O Father, Lord of heaven and earth, that Thou didst hide these things from the wise and intelligent and didst reveal them to babes. Yes, Father, for thus it was well pleasing in Thy sight. All things have been handed over to Me by My Father; and no one knows the Son, except the Father; nor does anyone know the Father, except the Son, and anyone to whom the Son wills to reveal Him" (Matthew 11:25-27).

> Now when Jesus came into the district of Caesarea Philippi, He began asking His disciples, saying, "Who do people say that the Son of Man is?" And they said, "Some say John the Baptist; and others, Elijah; but still others, Jeremiah, or one of the prophets." He said to them, "But who do you say that I am?" And Simon Peter answered and said, "Thou art the Christ, the Son of the living God." And Jesus answered and said to him, "Blessed are you, Simon Barjona, because flesh and blood did not reveal this to you, but My Father who is in heaven" (Matthew 16:13-17).

> "...And other seed fell into the good soil, and grew up, and produced a crop a hundred times as great." As He said these things, He would call out, "He who has ears to hear, let him hear." And His disciples began questioning Him as to what this parable might be. And He said, "To you it has been granted to know the mysteries of the kingdom of God, but to the rest it is in parables, in order that SEEING THEY MAY NOT SEE, AND HEARING THEY MAY NOT UNDERSTAND (Luke 8:8-10).

REVELATION

The last book of the Bible is aptly named. It is a revelation of what is to come. In the previous passages Jesus highlights the concept of revelation. In Matthew 11 He makes several points:

❖ God has deliberately hidden things from people.

❖ They will not be discovered on the basis of wisdom or intelligence.

- ❖ They will be made known to babes—those who seem least likely to receive them.

- ❖ This is God's best plan.

- ❖ God is made known only through Jesus.

- ❖ God is made known only by revelation. Jesus is the revelation of the Father on Earth.

One essential aspect of the New Testament is the idea that things are hidden. When Jesus was born in human form, those who were looking for Him and expecting Him failed to see Him when He arrived. The Gospels reveal the life of Jesus as one totally misunderstood by the majority of the Jews of the day. It is summed up in one short sentence in John 1:11: *"He came to His own, and those who were His own did not receive Him."* He was sent of the Father; Jesus came and did the Father's will. Although they were looking for Him, many rejected Him when they saw Him.

One very real example of this preconceived perception is when Jesus began His ministry (having been baptized by John the Baptist, filled with the Spirit, and tempted by the devil in the wilderness) and returned to His hometown of Nazareth. He taught in the synagogue and as He spoke, He suggested that the Jewish nation had not been so special as they thought, given some of the things God did for non-Jews in the Old Testament. Jesus was teaching in the power of the Spirit. Yet the people only recognized what they had known all their lives:

> *And all were speaking well of Him, and wondering at the gracious words which were falling from His lips; and they were saying, "Is this not Joseph's son?"* (Luke 4:22).

They saw the son of Joseph—they did not recognize the Son of God. Yet Jesus was different. What He was saying was new. It challenged. They reacted badly to Him.

Why? Why did they fail to see who He was? The truth is that He (His true identity) was hidden by the Father. The circumstances of His birth did not suggest to the Jewish mind that this was the promised son of David. Jewish tradition said that nothing good could come out of Nazareth, the place where He lived. His teaching caused theological minds to see Him as blasphemous. Ironically, that was the basis they used to condemn Him to the Cross.

Again we must ask, why? What *was* God's purpose? The answer is found in Matthew 11:27—Jesus has to *reveal* the Father to people for Him to be known. Unless revelation comes via Jesus from the Father, people will not recognize Him. This is why Jesus said to Nicodemus *"you must be born again."* Receiving the Truth (Jesus Himself) was and is to be by revelation and experience of the Holy Spirit. That is how each one of us entered into the Truth realm. We received revelation and experienced God's presence. It all happened through the Holy Spirit.

All of this helps us to understand the dialogue between Jesus and Peter written in Matthew 16. First of all, Jesus brings a contrast between what men say and what His followers say. *Who do men say I am?...who do you say I am?* Jesus has not made Himself known to the people. Any understanding about the real Jesus will come only by revelation. The answer to the two questions helps us understand how God operates. The disciples tell Jesus that people think He is John the Baptist, Elijah, Jeremiah or one of the prophets. These are not bad answers in that there is recognition of a godly man. However, these answers are wrong. The source is wrong—it is human. It is based on what is seen and heard. The correct answer is by revelation, not guesswork or mind games! To reduce Jesus to the level of a prophet does not allow Him to be Savior. If we see a prophet, we can only receive the reward of a prophet.

So when Peter says Jesus is the Christ, the Son of the living God, he is speaking from another, non-human, source. He is confident. He's not guessing. Why is he so confident? Why does he not say *I think you might be...?* Why is he not debating himself? He doesn't even discuss it with the others. He states his own conviction without hesitation.

Jesus explains for us all—and the other disciples—Peter's confidence as well as his answer. The source of his answer was not his *flesh* (the natural man). It was not a calculated response. The reply came from the revelation he received. It came from the Father. So Jesus pronounced Peter *blessed.* Revelation brings blessing. Pure theology is not simply found in academic studies. It is not discovered in the local church Bible study alone. It is not necessarily to be found because we sit under anointed ministry.

Revelation is revealed because we become and live as Spirit people. We can all sit in a good Bible study or under a great ministry and not receive revelation. We can also sit under the teaching of someone who is not explaining the Truth and yet still receive revelation—as happened with me concerning speaking in tongues. Revelation comes to the heart of anyone who is alert to the Spirit of Truth. It is His presence that is paramount if we are to enter into more of the Truth.

For example, after David sinned with Bathsheeba, he repented, and then expressed this important truth: *Behold, Thou dost desire truth in the innermost being, and in the hidden part Thou wilt make me know wisdom* (Ps. 51:6). The mind is not the seat of God's Truth. The place of God's Truth is the heart or inmost being. So the apostle Peter received Truth in his inmost being; it was *revealed* to him.

Knowing this helps us understand what Paul told the church in Corinth:

> *I ask that when I am present I may not be bold with the confidence with which I propose to be courageous against some, who regard us as if we walked according to the flesh. For though we walk in the flesh, we do not war according to the flesh, for the weapons of our warfare are not of the flesh, but divinely powerful for the destruction of fortresses. We are destroying speculations and every lofty thing raised up against the knowledge of God, and we are taking every thought captive to the obedience of Christ,* (2 Corinthians 10:2-5).

The flesh—human nature—does not of itself express the Truth. That's because God's Truth is only given and received through the Spirit of Truth and never by human understanding. Martin Luther obtained truth when it was revealed to him by the Spirit.[1] He knew the teaching from the Scripture, but it was the Spirit who gave him the revelation of the passage he already knew! Only the Sprit can bring life to words and produce revelation. John Wesley found his heart *strangely warmed* as the Spirit revealed the Gospel to him.[2]

Do you want to know the Truth today? It won't come just because you read a really good Christian book or even the Bible. It comes by the Spirit. Let the Spirit open the Truth to you. Take time in God's presence.

This way of living and receiving Truth remains essential to us no matter how long we have been believers. Paul wrote to the Galatian church: *"Are you so foolish? Having begun by the Spirit, are you now being perfected by the flesh?"* (Gal. 3:3). We must remain in the Spirit. Once we have entered the spiritual realm because we are born *of the Spirit*, we continue to learn in the same way. Note these verses:

> *As you therefore have received Christ Jesus the Lord, so walk in Him, having been firmly rooted and now being built up in Him and established in your faith, just as you were instructed, and overflowing with gratitude. See to it that no one takes you captive through philosophy and empty deception, according to the tradition of men, according to the elementary principles of the world, rather than according to Christ* (Col. 2:6-8).

Here are two totally opposed ways of moving ahead in life. The human way involves tradition, culture, thought, and philosophy. It's the way children are taught in school. This way is based on the fallen human nature and is rooted in sin. In the passage from Colossians, Paul tells us to *"continue in the way we received Jesus."* That's through new birth and by the Spirit through revelation. A famous line from a movie says, *"You can't handle the truth."*[3] Well, you can't handle the truth unless you receive it by revelation from the Holy Spirit. That's why there have always been so many disputes about doctrine.

Perhaps we have been too keen in the past to accept things just as they are. The Spirit of God is not satisfied with the status quo. Creation waits for the revealing of the children of God (you and me) that's part of the reason the Holy Spirit is still active on planet Earth. Is He active in us, today? He wants to bring daily ongoing revelation to us. Our part? That's easy! Just stay in the Spirit:

> *Therefore be careful how you walk, not as unwise men, but as wise, making the most of your time, because the days are evil. So then do not be foolish, but understand what the will of the Lord is. And do not one another in psalms and hymns and spiritual songs, singing and making melody with your heart to the Lord; always giving thanks for all things in the name of our Lord Jesus get drunk with wine, for that is dissipation, but be filled with the Spirit, speaking*

to Christ to God, even the Father; and be subject to one another in the fear of Christ (Ephesians 5:15-21).

Note that this passage also talks about how we walk and stay filled with Spirit because it is God's will. How is this accomplished?

- ❖ Stay in an attitude of worship and praise.

- ❖ Have others at the forefront of your priorities, over your own, in your standing before God.

- ❖ Remain humble.

Living with a servant attitude helps safeguard the Truth in us. We can't be worshipful, humble, and *reactionary!* There is ongoing victory in living as God tells us. The weapons of our warfare are not natural but they are effective! Consider this passage from First Peter 5:8-9:

> *Be of sober spirit, be on the alert. Your adversary, the devil, prowls about like a roaring lion, seeking someone to devour. But resist him, firm in your faith, knowing that the same experiences of suffering are being accomplished by your brethren who are in the world.*

So we are to be sober and alert in the Spirit. By the Spirit we overcome the enemy. In order to do that we must remain filled.

ENDNOTES

1. Tim Dowley, *Eerdmans' Handbook to the History of Christianity* (Grand Rapids, MI: Eerdmans, 1977), 364.

2. John Wesley, *Journal of John Wesley* (Chicago, IL: Moody Press, 1951), May 24, 1738.

3. Jack Nicholson, in *A Few Good Men* (1992), Columbia Pictures.

Chapter Four

SERMON ON THE MOUNT

Some of the greatest teaching of Jesus is found in the early chapters of Matthew's Gospel, known as the Sermon on the Mount. This teaching is fundamental to knowing Jesus while He was on the earth and to understand why His teaching was so different from that of the Pharisees and other religious leaders of the day.

One verse in particular is especially helpful to understand how the Sermon on the Mount applies to us today:

> *...the love of God has been poured out within our hearts through the Holy Spirit who was given to us* (Romans 5:5).

A great act of God took place when each of us became born again. God set His love in place *in our hearts.* That love in our hearts is the basis of the now relationship Jesus brought to us from Heaven. The heart is the seat of love. God made it possible for us to love as He loves by imparting His own love into our hearts, not just our feelings. When we recognize this, then we can understand the Sermon on the Mount more completely.

This particular passage of the Sermon of Jesus is known as *the Beatitudes:*

And when He saw the multitudes, He went up on the mountain; and after He sat down, His disciples came to Him. And opening His mouth He began to teach them, saying, "Blessed are the poor in spirit, for theirs is the kingdom of heaven. Blessed are those who mourn, for they shall be comforted. Blessed are the gentle, for they shall inherit the earth. Blessed are those who hunger and thirst for righteousness, for they shall be satisfied. Blessed are the merciful, for they shall receive mercy. Blessed are the pure in heart, for they shall see God. Blessed are the peacemakers, for they shall be called sons of God. Blessed are those who have been persecuted for the sake of righteousness, for theirs is the kingdom of heaven. Blessed are you when men cast insults at you, and persecute you, and say all kinds of evil against you falsely, on account of Me. Rejoice, and be glad, for your reward in heaven is great, for so they persecuted the prophets who were before you (Matthew 5:1-12).

These truths are based in the heart, not the mind. They are heart choices. They concern character, the type of person we choose to be. The Beatitudes have been misunderstood and misinterpreted because many have taken a legalistic approach to understanding them. We tend to study with the mind rather than take the truths to heart.

The word *beatitude* has to do with *blessing*. The word blessing really means "happiness." The happy state Jesus talks has to do with our relationship with God.

1. *Poor in Spirit* concerns a permanent recognition that in ourselves we are not adequate. We need the presence and input of the Holy Spirit. It is a decision of the heart to allow the Spirit to bring the rule of God—the Kingdom of Heaven—within us; we belong there.

2. *Those who mourn* make a choice. As a result of my closeness with God, I decide to mourn with Him. I also mourn with those who mourn. I am identifying with God's own heart. My choice is to be spiritually sensitive to God and what He wants.

3. *The meek* are not those who grovel. They have nothing to prove to anyone. They are what they are. They do not become boastful. They are not competitive. Again, it is a choice of the heart.

4. *Hungering and thirsting after righteousness.* We do not strive to obtain righteousness for ourselves. We realize that we cannot achieve it. Hunger and thirst for ongoing righteousness is in the depths of our hearts. We live in the righteousness that is achieved only through grace. We are never complacent about our walk in life either before God or people. We yearn for improvement.

5. *Merciful* is again a choice of the heart. There are many times when justice cries for judgment. Mercy calls out for forgiveness, a second chance. We are not operating in any way under Law—this has to do entirely with grace. It is a heart decision to be and do the best for the other person. This truth is evident throughout the Beatitudes. When we operate at this heart level, we are moving in genuine sowing and reaping of Kingdom values.

6. *Pure in heart* obviously talks of heart truth. Purity has to do with motive. Sometimes an outward appearance is good, but the heart motive is deceitful. Purity in heart is being like Nathaniel—there is no guile. (See John 1:47.) God sees the heart. The result of purity in heart is that we shall see Him.

In today's world, every one of the Beatitude phrases is considered a weakness. Unfortunately, people are caught up in the need for self-assurance and presenting a strong image toward others—even their friends. But true friendship and relationships don't work like that.

Human reality is based on our need for God and for one another. The character portrayed in the Beatitudes is one that expresses the desire to change for the better. Such people do not have a selfish ambition to be the strongest or best. Their primary focus is God. The second one is others, not self. These verses foreshadow the frequently repeated commandment to *love God and to love others as you do yourself.*

Verses immediately following the Beatitudes speak of God's people as salt and light. The salt of the earth refers to those who bring influence from God and savor the world, influencing people for the better. The phrase referring to believers as the light of the world speaks similarly. Light cannot be seen—we can only see its effect. As God's people we shed light into the world. But the source is internal. It's in our hearts. It's not some kind of torch that we are holding! So the heart is the place where God has placed His love in the believer. It is also the seat of Truth, the place where God's salt and light are established in each one of us. The heart, therefore, is key to all that follows in this great passage of the teaching of Jesus known as the Sermon on the Mount. Teaching speaks to the heart. Truth is lived from the heart.

Knowing and establishing this heart Truth also helps us to understand more of the other statements made by Jesus. I believe this Sermon is the hallmark of what Jesus taught and did while He was here on earth.

Jesus establishes the place of the Law through His teachings:

❖ He has not come to abolish the Law or the Prophets; He came to fulfill them. (See Matthew 5:17.)

❖ All the Law will be accomplished. (See Matthew 5:18.)

❖ These commandments cannot be cancelled. (Ibid.)

❖ The greatest in the Kingdom is the one who keeps and teaches them. (See Matthew 7:24; 18:1-4.)

❖ Our righteousness must surpass that of the Pharisees. (See Matthew 5:20.)

When we read these verses we may ask, *"Can anyone at all get saved"?* Yet we know Jesus came to save us. Jesus is really saying the Law will always stand in place for those who seek to live by it. He's also making the point that it is possible to live a level of righteousness beyond that of the Pharisees—teachers of the Law! In the New Testament, criticism of the Pharisees has to do with their hypocrisy. They talked what they did not walk. Their teaching was not internalized in their own lives. This is the hallmark of hypocrisy. Jesus did not live a hypocritical life. He spoke as from Heaven. He spoke as He was. He was the Word made flesh. Therefore He did not teach like the

Pharisees. His teaching was based on internal reality. That reality came from His experience of His Father. In other words, Jesus taught what He experienced. We should do the same.

So the teaching of Jesus has to do with what we are, internally. In His sermon He says *you are* the salt of the earth, the light of the world. What I am comes out at home, when I'm working, when I preach, and even in everyday conversations. Equally, what we are internally is also there in us to affect those around us—like salt and light.

PERSONAL LIFE

Jesus goes on to talk of specific situations in life. His remarks are startling in how He perceives the Law and the Commandments.

1. *Murder as Sin.*

> *You have heard that the ancients were told, 'YOU SHALL NOT COMMIT MURDER' and 'Whoever commits murder shall be liable to the court.' But I say to you that everyone who is angry with his brother shall be guilty before the court; and whoever shall say to his brother, 'Raca,' shall be guilty before the supreme court; and whoever shall say, 'You fool,' shall be guilty enough to go into the fiery hell. If therefore you are presenting your offering at the altar, and there remember that your brother has something against you, leave your offering there before the altar, and go your way; first be reconciled to your brother, and then come and present your offering* (Matthew 5:21-24).

Under the Law and in the life of God's people in Old Testament times, murder was, as it remains today in national and international law, the decision to, and actual deed of, killing someone. Jesus, in this statement, takes the meaning much further. Anger, He says, is at the source of murder. This is true from the beginning. When Cain murdered Abel, it was the result of his anger. The reason Cain became a murderer was not because of Abel. He was really angry with God because He had not received Cain's offering. In any case, God was generous in His comments to Cain: Then the LORD said to Cain, **"Why are you angry? And why has your countenance fallen? If you do well, will not your countenance be lifted up? And if you do not do well, sin is crouching at the door; and its desire is for you, but you must master it"** (Gen. 4:6,7).

This is an early example of God's grace. Cain could still find acceptability before God. It was his anger that caused him not to pursue God. That anger was turned against his brother, probably because Abel's offering was received when his own was not. The point is that the outward deed results from the internal workings (anger). This is Jesus' point in Matthew 5—murder is from the heart.

Words can also be murderous. Jesus tells us that when we say *you good-for-nothing* or *you fool* our words alone are sufficient to commit us to hell. People often say *I never did anyone any harm.* When they talk that way, they speak of deeds. Our words are also powerful and very destructive. What we speak from the heart affects the heart of the person we talk with—whether we are saying good or bad things. This means that there is fruit of our words in the lives of those we speak with.

But Jesus also gives us the solution. The way to help ourselves—don't let issues fester in your heart. Sort them out. *Leave your offering before the altar.* Even if you are a preacher, don't let your preaching gift take priority over sorting out the problem. When preachers fail to do this, our hearts speak differently from the words we say to people to help them. I'm sorry, but that's just like what the Pharisees did! The Truth is not the Truth if it is not in the heart of the speaker but only on his lips.

When things go wrong between us and someone else, we should always seek to settle things. It's important. It keeps our hearts pure. We should not seek the courts to settle a matter unless it's absolutely necessary. In Matthew 18 Jesus says that the final place to go, when the issue is with another believer, is the church. The legal courts are the place of murder; we assassinate the character of the other person. I know of a situation when church leaders who were meeting together became so angry that one of the men threatened to take the others to court! This is so far from what Jesus wants in His Church. We don't stay angry; we don't threaten others with court action. We move in the grace and righteousness that's in our hearts.

2. *Adultery.*

The sins of adultery and general unlawful sexual acts have troubled the church for centuries. This is the area satan can hurt God's people—especially through their leaders. It's also an area of great controversy. Let's note what Jesus actually says:

You have heard that it was said, 'YOU SHALL NOT COMMIT ADUL-TERY'; but I say to you, that everyone who looks on a woman to lust for her has committed adultery with her already in his heart. And if your right eye makes you stumble, tear it out, and throw it from you; for it is better for you that one of the parts of your body perish, than for your whole body to be thrown into hell. And if your right hand makes you stumble, cut it off, and throw it from you; for it is better for you that one of the parts of your body perish, than for your whole body to go into hell. And it was said, 'WHOEVER SENDS HIS WIFE AWAY, LET HIM GIVE HER A CERTIFICATE OF DI-VORCE'; but I say to you that everyone who divorces his wife, except for the cause of unchastity, makes her commit adultery; and whoever marries a di-vorced woman commits adultery (Matthew 5:27-32).

As with murder, Jesus is not talking about the act of adultery. If He had been, He would have dealt with the woman caught in the act of adultery very differently later (see John 8:3-11). The issue was not the sexual act. Jesus was, and remains, consistent. The issue with the woman was her *heart;* she remained before Jesus when her accusers had departed. She trusted Him in spite of the clear evidence of her sin—and Jesus did not dis-appoint her faith.

Jesus refers to a man committing adultery *in his heart* (see Matt. 5:28). Sin is internal. It may become an act eventually, but its *source* is in the heart. As we have been discussing, the whole matter of Truth lies within the heart; it's also the seat of sin.

The thought of sexual acts is revealed in two ways; through the eyes and touch. Jesus therefore talks of tearing out your eye and of cutting off your hand if either causes you to stumble. These are real clues. Jesus is referring to the Law when He speaks of cutting off the hand (see Deut. 25:11,12). This passage of His sermon is concerning the Law—He is establishing the Law be-yond the deed. The Law is broken in the heart first. The eye and the hand can cause sin to occur, but only after the heart goes there.

Any adult male reading the teachings of Jesus concerning this sin, will probably conclude that he has at some stage in life committed adultery in the eyes of the Law. He cannot redeem himself. The Law brings condem-nation. That condemnation comes in the heart because there is no Truth setting us free. All we know is guilt because we do not know the Truth. Many young men have talked with me over the years, struggling because they did not know the difference between Law and Grace. Grace provides the way out of the guilt into the place of victory.

3. *Divorce.*

Considering what you just read, Jesus' words concerning divorce (see Matt. 5:31,32) are in the context of the Law, not the church. Divorce outside what the Law allowed causes the woman to commit adultery. As far as Jesus is concerned in what He says here, there is no act required; adultery can apply to the woman simply because she and her husband are separated. That is His interpretation of the Law.

This is important because we cannot use these verses as part of our understanding of Jesus' view on divorce. They speak rather of His view of the Law. Therefore we cannot apply His words here to situations that occur within the people of God where grace is applied, not the Law.

OTHER MATTERS

Throughout the rest of His teaching in this Sermon on the Mount, Jesus talks of the life lived under and in the Grace of God. We do not look for retribution, living on a tit-for-tat basis. Others do not reap the bad seed they sow into our lives, because we allow the Truth to abide in us and therefore sow better things back into them. That's why Jesus says *"love your enemies"* (Matt. 5:44).

So the inward life in relationship with God is what He looks for. We do not do good so others see our righteousness (see Matt. 6:1). Our real prayer life is in the *secret place* (Matt. 6:4). Prayer is Truth. Truth is inward, personal. What is seen is the fruit, not the action.

Forgiveness is crucial to this life with God. His Truth is in us through His forgiveness (Matt. 6:14,15). What He has sown into us, we then sow into others. If we fail to forgive, our integrity with God is lost. What we have freely received we fail to give freely. Truth is only Truth in us when we live it. The Kingdom has nothing to do with the idea that *I'm alright.* It considers God first, then others. Every benefit of God in us is incorruptible seed. It is sown into us so that it fills our world. God's Truth lives; if it is in us, then it is active in our lives and sown, still incorruptible, from us into others.

Our lives are to be based in the unseen realm of the Kingdom. Prayer is private; so too is fasting. We lay up treasure in Heaven, not on earth. Since God's Truth is in us, we are in a place of peace under His rule. Inward contentment leaves no room for anxiety. We are blessed. You see we have to (many have failed to notice this) go back to the beginning of the Sermon. We are blessed because with the Truth in us we become, inwardly, those who live in the atmosphere where we are:

❖ Poor in spirit. We are and have nothing of ourselves. We have nothing to prove to others.

❖ Those who mourn. We long to see others coming out of their deathly existence.

❖ Gentle. We live within the nature of God in us. We are not given to violence.

❖ Hunger and thirst. Inwardly, we look for more from God. Our desire is for righteousness, Truth in the inward parts.

❖ Merciful. We constantly operate in forgiveness. We want to move in it for the sake of others. Our own relationship with God also depends on it.

❖ Pure in heart. Our heart is key to all we do. The purity of heart speaks of motive. We are not deceitful.

❖ Peacemakers. We make peace for the sake of others. Truth-based peacemakers do not seek their own benefit. That is how the Truth operated in Jesus. That's also how it should work through us.

❖ Persecuted. Suffering (as He did) for the sake of others and not trying to justify ourselves.

It's impossible to live as those justified by God and then seek to justify ourselves. There are many of God's people who fail to live in the realm of inner Truth. Through the presence of the Holy Spirit in us, we are justified before God. We do not need to justify ourselves before people! I have talked with leaders who speak of unfairness, trying to justify themselves when they got something wrong and tried to blame others. Inward Truth is what counts. When issues arise, Jesus tells us to win our brother, not the argument (see Matt. 18:15)!

You see, it's the inward integrity of the Truth of God in us, that seed sown in us, which manifests fruit. Recently I talked with someone who was unhappy with me. He was angry. I asked for his forgiveness. For some time after, he was blown away. It was the first time anyone had asked for forgiveness! This is someone who has been a Christian for years. Let's be winners—winners of people, not debates or arguments. Win your brother. If you can't attempt to do that, you will never win the world. People are looking for integrity in the church; unfortunately they see something that is closer to hypocrisy.

We can change; we can live it. Jesus told us we can. He is our example. He went to the Cross to win as the perfect mediator: but He did not win for Himself. His victory over sin was first in obedience to His Father. He won the victory for God by dealing that fatal blow to the devil when He paid the price for the sins of the whole world. This all pleased the Father and Jesus always does the Father's will. Jesus' integrity is not just what He did; it is the fruit of it.

That victory is also for us. Everyone who turns and believes in Jesus receives the promise of God. So Jesus' death is a victory for us too. It is a total win-win situation. As we became born again the Holy Spirit brought to us that victory over sin as a response from God to our faith (not our own righteousness). The same Spirit also brings to us the integrity of God, His Truth because the Holy Spirit is the Spirit of Truth. As a result, fruit appears in and through our lives, just as it did with Jesus, This may not be to the same extent, but it is the same Spirit!

This means we have to undo the literalist teaching found among the Pharisees in the times of the New Testament. It is important to do this because there still exists within the broad Church of God a literalist and legalistic approach to the outworking of the Scriptures in our lives. Truth in the inward parts is a result of the working of God's Spirit in us.

Chapter Five

TRUTH IS FRUIT

Jesus never appreciated lip service. I wonder how many of us have said things without really meaning them—probably all of us. We can sing the words of the songs and say *"hallelujah"* or *"amen,"* without any meaning to us. We can pray and say at the end, *"through Jesus Christ our Lord"* but if there is no faith, it carries no weight. If we say, *"He is Lord"* it doesn't make Jesus become our Lord. Words are not enough.

Let's look at what Jesus is saying in Matthew 7:21-23:

> *Not everyone who says to Me, 'Lord, Lord,' will enter the kingdom of heaven;*
> *but he who does the will of My Father who is in heaven. Many will say to Me*
> *on that day, 'Lord, Lord, did we not prophesy in Your name, and in Your name*
> *cast out demons, and in Your name perform many miracles?' And then I will*
> *declare to them, 'I never knew you; DEPART FROM ME, YOU WHO*
> *PRACTICE LAWLESSNESS.'*

This is one of the most radical of Jesus' teachings. Why would Jesus say such things? What was He teaching us? I believe it refers to the demons speaking things, which were true, *but the source was wrong.* We too can speak things from a wrong source. This would include being inspired by:

❖ Demonic influence (that happened to Peter!).

❖ Motivation of the flesh (the human spirit).

❖ The words of others (their flesh).

All of these wrong sources operate outside our experience of God. They interfere with the leading of the Spirit. Yet God has given us the right to move in the power of the Spirit. He has also enabled us to be led by the Spirit. The question is *how can we improve?*

I believe the answer lies in the words of Jesus quoted in John's Gospel where He said *I do nothing on my own initiative.* Everything He said and did was as a direct result of His experience of the Father. It seems to me we often fail to submit. We enjoy the power but fail to submit it to the wisdom of God or the prompting of the Holy Spirit.

Before I go rushing ahead, I must make something very clear. Just because something was successful done one way, on one occasion doesn't mean:

❖ The Holy Spirit will always lead us in the same way.

❖ That is our ministry.

❖ God will always want it done that way by others too.

❖ We are always anointed to do it the same way.

❖ We are in a season of moving in those things.

The *now* of God for every individual is based on our now experience of Him. We must not look for set patterns; we must look for God, experience Him, and do what He is saying to us, even when it doesn't make any sense to us.

Here's a key verse to help: *"But a natural man does not accept the things of the Spirit of God; for they are foolishness to him, and he cannot understand them, because they are spiritually appraised"* (1 Cor. 2:14).

We are raised, we interact with our families and friends; we are educated to operate in life on the basis of logic. This process does not work in the Spirit world. If it did, the Pharisees would have never needed to ask Jesus a question and the people would have always understood what He was saying. That was not the case. What Jesus said needed to be interpreted in terms of the Sprit, not logic. The same is true today. We can only understand the acts of God through our experience of Him.

Returning to the passage from Matthew 7, this statement is essential to our salvation: *we cannot enter the Kingdom of Heaven based on success in prophecy, casting out demons or moving in miracle power.* It is important to clearly understand that identity in the Kingdom of God is through the heart, not the things done. Obviously, it's also dangerous if we hear something that sounds good but is not based on the other person's now experience of God. How do we know? How can we decide?

First of all, as spiritual people we should have some level of discerning. Sometimes it's easy to know that there's something wrong about what's just been done or seen. Maybe we can't explain it but we just know in our hearts it's not right. God also helps His people when things are not so easily detected. In First Corinthians 12, Paul lists some gifts of the Holy Spirit. These include the gift of discerning of spirits. At certain times some people may spot something in the Spirit, which is not evident to all. In those cases, we need to learn to recognize when God is moving in a special way through someone. Here's an example:

In the early church people sold possessions, land, and houses to cater for the church in Jerusalem (see Acts 5). One couple in particular (Ananias and Sapphira) is mentioned in connection with this practice. They sold some property but kept some of the money for themselves and only brought part to the apostles. Peter challenged Ananias who lied and stated that the money he brought was the full amount. Peter then asked him why satan had put it into his heart to lie to the Holy Spirit. Peter spoke on and Ananias fell to the ground and died. Then his wife died.

It was only by the Spirit that Peter knew Ananias and Sapphira only brought a portion of the money and that they had agreed to *lie to the Holy Spirit.* The Holy Spirit is the Spirit of Truth; He detects lying. To the outward appearance, what Ananias and Sapphira did was good. It was helping the church. The problem was their motivation. The source was satanic. Peter knew the Truth only because he was experiencing God there and then. He had no other way of knowing. Later he dealt with Simon the sorcerer very differently because the source was the human spirit, not the demonic (see Acts 8). It is important to understand:

- ❖ The various spirits (human, demonic and Holy Spirit) operating in the spiritual realm.

- ❖ The importance of discerning by the Holy Spirit in all situations and at all times.

- ❖ The need to live in a constant experience of God.

We have already noted that in Matthew 7 Jesus tells us that accurate prophecy, moving in miracles, and casting out demons are not in themselves sufficient to enter the Kingdom of Heaven. What He stresses we need instead (or before we move in those things) is to know Him. This again speaks to us of the need for intimacy with the Father, Jesus, and the Holy Spirit. It is only on the basis of knowing them in the now that we should move out in supernatural power. Otherwise we are not operating in the Truth. Knowing them requires listening for the voice of the Spirit; He will tell us what to do and how to do it. We really need to listen all the time. The Bible is clear: *"he who has an ear, let him hear what the Spirit is saying to the church"* (Revelation 2:7,11,17,29; 3:6,13,22). So we need to be hearing. We need to hear now! Jesus told us to be on the alert, to watch and pray. So often we don't seem to manage it. We just need to practice being in the Spirit, whether we are in a time of prayer or not. This is how we experience *the Truth that abides in us* (2 John 2); it is only by the Spirit.

Although I may move in some of these things about which I'm writing, I definitely don't claim to have "arrived." There are times when some senior leaders speak or act as though they were *it.* I'm still not sure today what *it* is. No matter how much we may feel we have it, we can't move on presumption. We need the *now* experiencing of God. One of the most grievous things we can experience is to see someone of great reputation (and rightly so) in later life operating on presumption and losing the sense of the Holy Spirit's leading.

Samson was one who responded in presumption. To me one of the saddest verses in Scripture is: *"he* [Samson] *did not know that the LORD had departed from him"* (Judg. 16:20).

He had moved so powerfully so many times. On this occasion, with his haircut off—and his relationship with God lost—the fruit was different. It's by the fruit we know. In the context of Samson, his relationship with Delilah and the Philistines, they all knew by the fruit that he had lost his anointing. It's for us to recognize the fruit, not just what the person has done previously. I wonder how many times we sit in conferences presuming that the person who is speaking still operates under the anointing he had when we last heard him.

THE SANDWICH

So with this Truth in mind, let's visualize a sandwich that has Matthew 7:21-23 in the center—the meat, if you like! The verses before constitute the top slice of meat: those coming after make up the bottom piece of meat. It's a whole sandwich—the Bread of Life surrounds it. We need to consume it all together to understand what Jesus was really saying.

The Top Slice—Prophecy and Truth

Matthew 7 verses 15-20 are the top slice of sandwich meat. It's obvious that these two passages of meat go together with verses 21-23 because of Jesus' own words. Notice what He says:

Beware of the false prophets, who come to you in sheep's clothing, but inwardly are ravenous wolves. ... You will know them by their fruits (vv. 15-20).

Not everyone who says to Me, 'Lord, Lord,' will enter the kingdom of heaven; but he who does the will of My Father who is in heaven. Many will say to Me on that day, 'Lord, Lord, did we not prophesy in Your name...' (vv. 21-23).

Verses 15-20 links directly with verses 21-23. The top slice talks of *false prophets;* the second speaks of those who will have claimed to prophesy in Jesus' Name and who will yet be rejected. In other words, both refer to prophecy falsehood.

This means that some who prophesy will be *ravenous wolves*. Even if they say what is true, they will be known *by their fruit and not what they actually said*. That fruit is produced in the listeners, not what was actually said. Prophecy in God is not just stating facts. True prophecy from the heart of God will:

❖ Reveal His heart.

❖ Reveal the validity of the person prophesying.

❖ Produce the right fruit in the lives of the listeners.

Now we must investigate what is the right kind of fruit. This depends on the situations as they arise. Sometimes a word from God will call for repentance. At other instances it may encourage the people to hold in faith in a current situation. Prophecy will contain within it the appropriate goals of God for His people both in the immediate and into the future.

But there's more than this to prophecy. When the Bible talks of fruit in the believer, it is speaking of faith and character. Simply said: you should expect to see fruit in someone (not necessarily only believers) as a result of a prophecy, which is from God, and given through a godly person. If no fruit, then there is an issue in the heart of those receiving the word.

The other verse to discuss in the light of prophecy is First Corinthians 14:3. Here we are told that prophecy is given for building up, encouragement, and comfort. Any or all of these three purposes for prophecy should result in the heart of the believers when genuine prophecy is given. This means that the word from God has to be delivered with His heart in that word in order for the prophecy to be from God in its fullness.

However, in Matthew 14, Jesus speaks of something else. It is to do with those who prophesied *falsely*. False prophecy has nothing to do with actual accuracy of word. The real issue is the source. Jesus speaks of false prophets as wolves—not exactly a blessing to the flock of God! Wolves bring destruction, worry, fear, and death for God's people. The fruit they bring into the lives of the believers is wrong and can be seen as wrong.

Perhaps you have sat in meetings and heard someone deliver something, which was clearly not from God, but the words spoken sounded ok. What was wrong was the heart motive of the person prophesying. You may have noticed there was no rise of faith in the meeting, all spiritual momentum was lost. Thankfully God always gives a way forward. His promises hold true. When a prophecy comes across contrary to that, then the prophecy must be weighed accordingly (see 1 Cor. 14:29). It should then be handled publicly.

Prophecy can only be given in the context of the speaker's immediate experience of God. If not, it is either from the human spirit (the more likely) or demonically inspired. In either case, the result in the heart of the hearer is not positive.

Prophecy is sowing. Depending on the source, the speaker either sows from the human spirit, the demonic, or the Holy Spirit. Whatever is sown produces fruit. It's by the fruit that we recognize the prophesying—and why the source is so important.

Jesus will say of those who prophesy falsely, *I never knew you; DEPART FROM ME,* He did not know them. There was no relationship. Where there is no relationship with Jesus, Truth will not be revealed from or to any of us. If we operate outside the Spirit, we do so separated from our relationship with God.

I have a good friend who met from time to time with another man we both know. Although the man was apparently saying good things, he did so from a heart of flesh. As a result wrong thoughts about me were provoked in my friend. He found himself starting to doubt my integrity. He had an unwarranted and illogical growing mistrust of me. Over a period of time my friend realized what was happening and stopped meeting the other man. The issues of doubt disappeared.

Motives of the heart are not superficial. They are not recognized by everyone. That's why Jesus didn't always let people know who He was and how He knew what was in men's hearts (see John 2:24-25). We need to make sure that we operate in the Spirit of God and stay in the Spirit. God will reveal to us what we need to know beyond what is obvious and visible.

Motives and heart source also touch on the whole issue of effective prayer. We need to be moving in a Spirit understanding of Truth. That's why Paul wrote: *"With all prayer and petition pray at all times in the Spirit"* (Eph. 6:18). If we are in the Spirit we will pray the right things.

Interestingly, this phrase immediately follows the passage Paul writes about putting on the whole armor of God. Living in the equipping of God helps keep us in the Spirit.

In a similar passage, Paul writes *"Pray without ceasing"* (1 Thess. 5:17). It's only when we take this phrase out of its isolation that we see what Paul is provoking:

> *Rejoice always; pray without ceasing; in everything give thanks; for this is God's will for you in Christ Jesus. Do not quench the Spirit*...(1 Thessalonians 5:16-19).

We can pray without ceasing. We can also quench the Spirit. If we remain rejoicing (practicing the presence of God, see Ps. 16:11), then we continue to be filled with the Holy Spirit (See Eph. 5:18-19). This means we are continually experiencing God. Truth is in the inward parts. According to the Thessalonian passage it's His will. True theology is the experience of God. It's internal. It's not just found in theological writings.

False prophecy badly affects our relationship with God. True prophecy provokes intimacy with Him, faith, encouragement, building up, and comfort in the hearer.

Finally, one more comment about prophecy. Although we have (in the context of the words of Jesus) dealt almost exclusively with false prophesying, we need to also examine the hearers of prophetic words where exactly the same principles of experiencing God apply. If I am not in tune with the Holy Spirit when a prophecy is given, I will fail to receive it, as I should because I am listening from the wrong heart. Jesus taught that it is from the heart that someone speaks. It is also true that those who listen to any communication need to do so from the right-heart, Holy Spirit basis. If I am listening on the basis of self (the flesh) or, worse still, under demonic influence, then I will not hear Father's heart, I will miss God's message. My response will be completely wrong.

Now the lower slice of the sandwich...

Truth Is Fruit

The Lower Slice

We need to be responsive listeners to what God says. With this in mind, let's look at the other slice of meat in our sandwich—verses 24-27 of Matthew 7. These are the lower slice of the passage.

> *Therefore everyone who hears these words of Mine, and acts upon them, may be compared to a wise man, who built his house upon the rock. And the rain descended, and the floods came, and the winds blew, and burst against that house; and yet it did not fall, for it had been founded upon the rock. And everyone who hears these words of Mine, and does not act upon them, will be like a foolish man, who built his house upon the sand. And the rain descended, and the floods came, and the winds blew, and burst against that house; and it fell, and great was its fall* (Matthew 7:24-27).

The first word, *therefore*, indicates that what follows refers to the previous passage, bringing further explanation. Jesus stresses the point about those who hear His words but do not *put them into practice.* They are building houses (their lives) on a foundation of sand. The previous verse tells us that it is important to know Him. We do not put His words into practice if we do not know Him. Back to basics—intimacy with Jesus through the Holy Spirit is fundamental. This is the only foundation for operating in the Truth.

It is possible to say, "I know Him" without doing what He says. If someone plans to live that way, well, it won't work. Consider again Jesus' words from Matthew 7: *"Not everyone who says to Me Lord, Lord will enter the kingdom of heaven; but he who does the will of My Father who is in heaven."* You see this is the answer. We might say to Him "Lord" but that doesn't make Him your Lord. Those who really see Him as Lord are those who hear His words and *act upon them.* Then they know Him as Lord, because they do what He says.

When I was a teenager, a neighbor woman in her 40s invited me to go on vacation with her and her nephew into Scotland to a farmhouse situated by a sea loch. She would stay in the house and we would camp on the grounds. When we arrived, she pointed us to a place she said was suitable to pitch the tent. I questioned whether the site was too close to a stream but she was convinced we would be fine.

I'm sure you can guess the rest of the story! That night, it rained and rained and there was a high tide. I woke up in the early hours of the morning soaking wet from fresh water pouring in the top of the tent, and salt water lapping at my feet. Everything was drenched and needed to be dried out. We decided to pitch the tent elsewhere.

Now that's not the end of the story. This neighbor lady had been trained as a ranger. She knew what she was talking about. But let me list the fruit of this slice of history:

- ❖ I didn't trust that neighbor again concerning these matters, and probably most others.

- ❖ I didn't trust her qualifications.

- ❖ I hated camping.

- ❖ I never went camping again.

- ❖ I didn't trust people who seemed to be experts in camping.

Here's the problem: History like this causes us to distrust. When a church leader wrongs us (yes, it does happen) then we assume all leaders are the same. The truth is this—you know each leader by the fruit of his life in yours, not your own history.

When it comes to Jesus, He doesn't say, "I'm the Boss"—but He is. He says what we need to do on the following basis:

- ❖ He knows what's best.

- ❖ He is always providing for our good.

- ❖ He never gets it wrong.

- ❖ He never lets us down.

- ❖ His grace toward us, not legalism.

- ❖ Forgiveness is enacted for our every mistake.

- ❖ If you don't do it, you'll learn the hard way.

If only church leaders were like this! They should be. You see if we are to be effective in our daily lives, then we must act upon the words of

Jesus. If we don't live like Him, we don't put into practice what He said. We are to learn of Him.

KNOWING HIM

So *how* do we know Him? Years ago, we used to say *if He isn't Lord of all, then He isn't Lord at all*. Such a view is based on Law. He wants to be Lord of our hearts first so He can bring His Lordship into the things we do. The first time Jesus spoke with Peter after he had denied Him, He did not speak at all of what Peter had done. The question was *do you love Me?* Jesus spoke of the heart, not the deed. With Ananias and Sapphira (see Acts 5), Peter identified the problem where satan had access to their hearts. In the case of Simon the sorcerer (see Acts 8), the issue was his heart was *not right with God*. If Jesus is Lord of the heart, then even when mistakes are made, there is a heart foundation of relationship that counts for more than successful prophecy, moving in miracles, giving money, and everything else we can name.

So this is why Jesus could talk of the day when He would say to people, in the context of judgment, *I never knew you*. From the moment we encounter Jesus, meet Him with faith, and respond to Him by repentance, we become born again. It's a heart operation. We come into intimacy with Jesus. As a result we start a process. From the presence of the Holy Spirit in the heart, we are transformed but we also continue to change. Knowing him makes us more like Him.

It is only then we *do* the works that are pleasing to God. This explains the importance of knowing Him. If I prophesy then it is on the basis of my knowing Him *at that time when I am prophesying*. If I am not operating by the Spirit then I have no right to be doing anything. To fail to operate in the Holy Spirit is, in effect, to operate in a wrong spirit. The inspirational source is wrong.

FRUIT

The lower slice also speaks of fruit. The wise and foolish men built houses that appeared at least to be similar, if not identical. Everything looked the same. The only difference was that the foolish man built more quickly. He probably seemed to be the better builder! The real difference between the two houses was in the unseen; it was below ground, out of sight.

I remember years ago when I was leading a church in England. Over a period of about 18 months, more than 30 people left the membership (I might add that at the same time more joined than actually left). One Sunday morning a woman in the church came to the front during the worship time to speak prophetically. She started talking about wanting to get her apples off the trees. Saturday was the only day she was able to do this and for two Saturdays consecutively it had rained all day. She went before God to complain. He told her *the good apples would stay on the trees.*

It was clearly a word to the church at the time—that the good was staying in the church. It also speaks to us now. Good fruit remains. Fruit produced by the right building is evidenced in the fact that the house stands during the time of testing. It has been built properly.

So the fruit of a good foundation is that the house remains standing. Fruit is not always immediate: but when it appears, it is the evidence of what is internal, unseen. That's so true of our lives. The Truth is lived first. It is internal and comes from a heart of integrity, with no other agenda than God's.

Here is another significant passage. Notice these verses from the words of Jesus in John 15:

> *I am the true vine, and My Father is the vinedresser. Every branch in Me that does not bear fruit, He takes away; and every branch that bears fruit, He prunes it, that it may bear more fruit. You are already clean because of the word, which I have spoken to you. Abide in Me, and I in you. As the branch cannot bear fruit of itself, unless it abides in the vine, so neither can you, unless you abide in Me. I am the vine, you are the branches; he who abides in Me, and I in him, he bears much fruit; for apart from Me you can do nothing. If anyone does not abide in Me, he is thrown away as a branch, and dries up; and they gather them, and cast them into the fire, and they are burned. If you abide in Me, and My words abide in you, ask whatever you wish, and it shall be done for you. By this is My Father glorified, that you bear much fruit, and so prove to be My disciples* (John 15:1-8).

Truth Is Fruit

Now to tie this fruit and sandwich meal together. In Matthew 7 Jesus told the disciples they would recognize true and false prophets *by their fruit.* In John 15 He says that fruit only comes from those who *abide in Him.* Abiding is more than a daily "quiet" time with God. Abiding has to do with *now*—all the time. We abide as part of the branches. Life flows from Him to us. If the life flow stops, things go terribly wrong.

I notice that when I buy flowers for my wife, she always cuts a short length off the bottom of the stems before putting them in a vase of water. She tells me that this ensures that air does not block the flow of water to the flower heads. Otherwise the flowers die and there's no fruit. It's the same with us. If we fail to abide in Christ, in the Vine, we lose the life flow. The fruit is lost and the work of God is brought into disrepute.

Loss of fruit brings disrepute to the name of Jesus. The greatest damage to the Kingdom of God occurs when His people operate in something other than their intimacy with Him—no matter how successful the praying or prophesying may be. Where there is bad fruit that is what others will notice. The Truth only comes from intimacy through the Holy Spirit. This is true theology—the continuous experience of God. Anything else produces bad fruit. It is sad to admit, but bad fruit has been part of the history of the church. God's people strayed; their doctrine became infected and bad fruit was produced.

When we seek to reach others, it's helpful to recognize that one mistake can undo a lot of good. Look how the news media enjoy expounding on things that go wrong. There are immediate consequences to our mistakes. That's why it's needful to stay in the Spirit. I hope we all realize that one mistake can undo a lifetime of ministry. It's nothing new. Many Old Testament kings departed from the Lord in later life. Every time, there was more bad fruit.

When Jesus told the story of the wise and foolish men building their houses, He revealed the time lapse between the completion of the building and when the evidence of what it was built on came into reality. This is the fruit of the foundation. Sometimes it takes a while for the fruit to be revealed.

Although I am no expert on plants (I possibly know a little more about fruit), it seems to me that a plant can be very vigorous, produce lots of colorful flowers, and yet produce little fruit. God brings His power into our lives and our ministries. If we stay in the Spirit, we continually recognize His goodness—and fruit is produced to His glory, not ours.

Our intimacy with God is that which brings the life flow of the Spirit to us. The quality of fruit is dependant on its source. As we consider Truth and Fruit, we cannot ignore the statement of Jesus *I am the **true** vine* (John 15:1). In this fact, He puts these two essential ingredients together—they both concern Him and come from Him. We cannot have truth-fruit without Jesus! If we do not know Him, we cannot move in the Truth of which He is the unique source.

It would be so easy if Jesus went on to say that we were the fruit. He doesn't. He tells us we are *the branches.* (See John 15:5.) This changes things. It heightens our profile and responsibility. We are those who tap into Jesus as the Truth life source. With Him as the vine, we are the life channels that carry life from the source so that the fruit is produced.

There are times when we ask God to do what He's given us responsibility for doing. We ask Him to keep us on the vine. God tells us that's our task, not His. John 15:4 says: *"Abide in Me, and I in you. As the branch cannot bear fruit of itself, unless it abides in the vine, so neither can you, unless you abide in Me."* So we need to stay connected to the truth-life source that is Jesus. As long as I am abiding in Him I am able to receive Truth. This means that unless I am abiding in Jesus, I am straying into error! Truth has to do with the center of our being. Theology is our *now* experience of God. True theology produces the right fruit because the study of God is meaningless unless we are abiding in Him. That kind of non-relational research is unhelpful because when we start on a purely academic basis, we operate outside the Truth that comes through relationship by the Spirit with God.

Abiding in Jesus is the place of answered prayer. Jesus said, *"If you abide in Me, and My words abide in you, ask whatever you wish, and it shall be done for you"* (John 15:7). Why is this the case? Because answered prayer is fruit in your life and into the world. Prayer is Truth communication between the believer and God. Prayer is only effective when we operate in this Truth, because this is where we experience God.

Jesus also said, *"Every branch in Me that does not bear fruit, He takes away; and every branch that bears fruit, He prunes it, that it may bear more fruit."* and *"If anyone does not abide in Me, he is thrown away as a branch, and dries up; and they gather them, and cast them into the fire, and they are burned"* (John 15:2,6).

These more controversial statements by Jesus suggest that God recognizes and deals with spiritual barrenness. Apparently, we can become "cut off" from the Truth. Perhaps this is the kind of thing that happened to King Saul, Judas Iscariot, or Ananias and Sapphira. All of them turned to deceitfulness.

Whatever your views may be on this matter, we are all required to guard our own lives. We cannot separate out different aspects of the way we should live; we also cannot try to identify different strengths as "my" fruit. According to the New Testament, there is one fruit of the Spirit; it has various aspects. We cannot pick and choose. When we abide in Christ and do His will—the fruit grows. How is it recognized? That's easy! Jesus said, *"By this is My Father glorified, that you bear much fruit, and so prove to be My disciples"* (John 15:8). This is the fruit fit for repentance. It causes God to be glorified.

Such abundant, quality fruit through us is achieved as we live selfless lives. Jesus also said, *"Truly, truly, I say to you, unless a grain of wheat falls into the earth and dies, it remains by itself alone; but if it dies, it bears much fruit"* (John 12:24). If we abide alone, outside Christ, we bear no fruit. So fruit is essential to the way fruit is recognized. We are all known by our fruit, not our abilities or certificates. They may help, but they are neutral as far as Truth is concerned.

There is so much that can be written to give evidence to what I am writing about Truth and fruit. The crucial question for us to ask ourselves, though, is: What evidence is there in lives and situations around us that we are bearing the right fruit to the glory of God? What goes on in our private lives will ultimately produce fruit in what is seen.

Part Three

The Acts of the Apostles

Chapter Six

PENTECOST

To further understand how the Truth came to the disciples of Jesus in Bible times, I turn to the Book of Acts. This particular book is one of the most exciting in the whole of the Bible. So much happens—so many changes take place. In the beginning of the Book of Acts, there is no Holy Spirit power among the apostles. By the end, the Holy Spirit is moving powerfully in local churches as well as through the apostles; the Gospel has been established in many nations, especially through Paul. What we need to examine here is *how the Truth was made known to the apostles.*

The beginning of Acts tells us that after He was raised from the dead, Jesus spent 40 days teaching the apostles about the Kingdom of God. We *must* wonder what was contained in the teaching. We have no evidence concerning what was said, however, it seems obvious that whatever Jesus taught the disciples had to be beyond what He had previously said to them. It also means that what we can now read about Jesus' teaching as is revealed to us in the Gospels does not contain His teaching on the Kingdom at this point. In His post-resurrection teaching, Jesus was preparing the twelve for something else, a new phase.

So the result of Jesus' teaching about the Kingdom was preparation for a new experience through information; there was no immediate change in disciples or what they did until the Day of Pentecost. We know this because after 40 days of teaching, they did nothing for seven weeks. Information was not enough—something more was required before they could effectively enter into ministry. This is the process Jesus went through as well. He entered into His ministry only after he had received the fullness of the Holy Spirit and then returned to Galilee *in the power of the Spirit*. He had plenty of information—He knew His Father. But He had to be filled with the Holy Spirit before He was released into genuine spiritual ministry.

So it was the same with the apostles. They did nothing until they received the fullness of the Spirit. They had to wait. They were not alone. Contrary to popular belief, there is nothing to suggest that they were in the upper room. In fact, it is more likely that they were in the temple area. The end of Acts chapter 2 tells us that they continued meeting in the temple. The place where they met had sufficient space for 120 people—ten times the number that met with Jesus in the upper room! Wherever they were, thousands of others heard the noise of them speaking in tongues and came running. They do not appear to have been behind closed doors, nor in a confined space.

The Pre-Spirit Situation

Decision-making

It also helps us if we consider some of the other aspects of the disciples' situation just prior to the coming of the Spirit on the Day of Pentecost. First of all there was no real spiritual dimension to their deliberations and decisions. They felt they should find a replacement for Judas Iscariot, and the decision was reached by drawing lots. I am not willing to debate the extent to which this decision was the will of God. In Old Testament times the drawing of lots was an acceptable method to find answers unobtainable by human reason (see Jonah 1:7). Some would say that Paul was the real replacement for Judas. Either way, the result is speculation rather than fact.

What *is* known is that later decisions of the same type were not made on the same basis; the process was more spiritual. The sending of Barnabas and

Saul (Paul) to fulfill their apostolic call was the result of a word from the Spirit (see Acts 13:1). The appointment of the men to oversee the distribution of food was by consultation with the people on the basis of character and spiritual endowment. The same can be said of the recognition of elders.

UNITY

Throughout the Bible there are frequent references to the importance of unity. United action is powerful. I recall a few years ago being in a hotel in North Wales, meeting a good friend, when about 20 young men (in their late teens) walked through the foyer. They were members of a foreign national youth soccer team. The presence they carried was amazing! Unity put into action carries power.

Prior to the coming of the Holy Spirit on the Day of Pentecost, there was unity. The Bible tells us that the 120 people were *all together in one place* (Acts 2:1). They had the teaching of Jesus, they had unity but they did not have the power. Jesus had told them to wait so as to receive the power of the Holy Spirit before they could be His witnesses (see Acts 1:8). Unity is ineffective unless it has power.

Power without unity is also not effective. It may work and success can be achieved; however, it remains true that it is not good for a man to be alone. Isolation while working under the anointing of God carries with it a different kind of weakness–vulnerability. Some may say they have unity. Others might say they have power. The Word of God says we need both.

The life and teachings of Jesus were marked by His authority and power. Both bore testimony to who He was. Teaching, moving in power, and expressing the authority of God in the way we are and live are all part of us communicating the Truth, just as He did.

THEY HEARD, THEY SAW, THEY CONQUERED

So when the Holy Spirit did come in all His fullness the disciples were in something of a public place, probably not expecting what actually happened. The sound came from heaven—a rushing mighty wind. Tongues of fire appeared on each of them. This was not stuff that could be understood in the mind. A new era was breaking out, one which would lead them to trust the Holy Spirit. This era would consist in an experience of the Holy Spirit leading them into both the Truth revealed and the realm of power.

They Heard

This new experience was beyond their inner feelings. As the Holy Spirit arrived, they first heard it, *"there came from heaven a noise like a violent, rushing wind"* (Acts 2:2). The sound was not imagined. It was important. If it was not, then Luke, the writer of the Book of Acts would never have mentioned it. They all heard it. It signified something. What they heard came from Heaven. It was new. It was experience, needed experience, because it would confirm what followed, and they later moved in the Spirit's power.

Why was it not expected? First of all it came suddenly. It took them by surprise. They had seen Spirit manifestations in the life of Jesus. They saw the dove descend on Him. They heard a voice from Heaven. They saw Him transfigured. The also saw His resurrected body and His ascension into Heaven.

But this time it was personal to them. They experienced the Spirit manifestations. This was *their* personal experience, not just their testimony to what they saw in Jesus' life. From this moment on their testimony could include what they experienced firsthand of the Spirit. The important word is *experience*. They had experienced the *presence* of the Holy Spirit when Jesus breathed on them after His resurrection (John 20:22). Now they were experiencing direct divine power and signs. This was the Spirit of Truth that Jesus had promised to them. Their experience of the Spirit was Truth. This was new. It was more than words; Truth lay in their experience of God.

The Day of Pentecost brought a new relationship between the believers and God. There are still churches today that view the experience of the Holy Spirit at Pentecost as a new destination—thinking that after people speak in tongues they have arrived. But Pentecost was not a terminus—it was a new start. It's the Pentecost experience that opens up the Spirit realm as the foundation for all that takes place in the Book of Acts. That's how things should still be today.

On the Day of Pentecost, Peter spoke with amazing revelation. It's possible that at least some of this came from the teaching of Jesus after His resurrection: but the results were far greater than any of the apostles had ever seen in their personal ministry. The message and its impact take us back to the personal words of Jesus in Matthew 16:13-19:

> *Now when Jesus came into the district of Caesarea Philippi, He began ask-ing His disciples, saying, "Who do people say that the Son of Man is?" And they said, "Some say John the Baptist; and others, Elijah; but still others, Je-remiah, or one of the prophets." He said to them, "But who do you say that I am?" And Simon Peter answered and said, "Thou art the Christ, the Son of the living God." And Jesus answered and said to him, "Blessed are you, Simon Barjona, because flesh and blood did not reveal this to you, but My Father who is in heaven. And I also say to you that you are Peter, and upon this rock I will build My church; and the gates of Hades shall not overpower it. I will give you the keys of the kingdom of heaven; and whatever you shall bind on earth shall be bound in heaven, and whatever you shall loose on earth shall be loosed in heaven."*

Who is the Son of Man? Jesus wanted the disciples to answer His ques-tion. Peter gave the right answer, *and Simon Peter answered and said, "Thou art the Christ, the Son of the living God...you are Peter, and upon this rock I will build My church...*(Matt. 16:16,18).

It is important to identify what, not who, the rock on which the church would be built. It was not Peter himself who was the rock because a few moments later, Jesus addressed him as satan.

But He turned and said to Peter, "Get behind Me, Satan! You are a stumbling block to Me; for you are not setting your mind on God's interests, but man's" (Matt. 16:23). The rock on which Jesus would build His Church is not satan for He said the gates of Hades would not be able to prevail against this church.

So what rock was Jesus referring to? It had to do with what Peter said—He recognized who Jesus was. Not only that, he had received the revelation directly from God. *The rock is the revelation of Jesus from the Father.* It is on this rock that Peter launched his apostolic ministry. On the Day of Pentecost he brought into being the church in Jerusalem. He was speak-ing from what he knew by the Spirit.

When we look at the life of Peter, we find that he is not highly educated. But when he and John were examined by the priest and Sadducees, those theologically trained men were challenged:

> *Now as they observed the confidence of Peter and John, and understood that they were uneducated and untrained men, they were marvelling, and began to recognize them as having been with Jesus. And seeing the man who had been healed standing with them, they had nothing to say in reply* (Acts 4:13-14).

Peter, clearly uneducated, spoke on the Day of Pentecost with great power and authority. Questions come to mind—all with the same answer:

❖ Where did the power come from?

❖ Where did Peter get his boldness?

❖ Why did 3,000 people become believers?

❖ How did this uneducated, theologically untrained man know and quote an Old Testament passage and prophet?

❖ How did a man who had denied Jesus three times and had lived in the fear of the Jews suddenly gain such boldness?

The one and only answer: by the Spirit.

This answer also explains the vast array of healings, miracles, and revelations that took place from Pentecost forward. This was an era when the Truth came by the Spirit. This is essential to our understanding of the Book of Acts. It is also key to the ongoing revelations, manifestations of God's power (and, frankly, its lack) across the centuries since then. The Truth came to Peter and the other apostles by the Spirit. We should still be receiving Truth in the same way today. Pentecost marked the end of intellectual study in order to receive the Truth. Jesus embodies the Truth and the Holy Spirit remains the Spirit of Truth. He has not changed in either function or nature. This neglected Truth is examined in more detail in the next chapter.

Chapter Seven

THE SPIRIT

Many people today understand that the Book of Acts in itself is only the *beginning*. The writer makes this clear in the first chapter and verse:

> *The first account I composed, Theophilus, about all that Jesus began to do and teach until the day when He was taken up, after He had by the Holy Spirit given orders to the apostles whom He had chosen* (Acts 1:1-2).

It is also noticeable that the Book of Acts tends to feel unfinished when reaching the end of it. It wouldn't make sense for Luke to write about continuing what he left undone, only to fail to finish the second book.

However, this book may feel unfinished because it's an account of something that began on the Day of Pentecost and continues today. The Holy Spirit has come and He is still here with us. His function hasn't changed. He is still guiding us into all Truth.

Notice John 14:16-17: *"And I will ask the Father, and He will give you another Helper, that He may be with you forever; that is the Spirit of truth, whom the world cannot receive, because it does not behold Him or know Him, but you know Him because He abides with you, and will be in you."* Jesus said He would be with you forever—He hasn't gone away. He is still with us, still doing what He said He would do.

We have not achieved the fullness of the Truth. It would be human arrogance either to say we don't need any more revelation or that academic study could somehow replace the work of the Holy Spirit. That is why the Book of Acts is still as important as ever. It teaches us how to go on receiving Truth—by the Spirit.

Not only is the Spirit still with us, He is *in* us. That's the level of intimacy that God wants to have with us. By giving us His Spirit He has made it possible for us to have unbroken fellowship—genuine intimacy with Him.

But unfortunately, fellowship has become a religious word. As believers, we can be present physically in a church meeting and yet be elsewhere in our thoughts. We often try to live two different lives and we forget that the Holy Spirit lives in us all the time. Fellowship means sharing. I wonder if it would help if, as with the Greek translation, *sharing* would be used instead of *fellowship.* Maybe then it would be easier to understand how God wants to restore His intimacy with us after Adam lost it (see Genesis 3). It would certainly help us get real about God instead of having that internal, maybe *infernal* on-off switch in us!

In John 14 Jesus said that the Spirit would be our helper. This is a staggering Truth. God the Holy Spirit lives in imperfect beings like you and me in order to help us! Perhaps we fail to realize just how much God Himself is our Helper. (Read Psalm 54:4.)

By His Spirit God:

- ❖ Wants intimacy with you so His Spirit lives in you. You can share life (fellowship) with Him all the time.

- ❖ Brings a plumb line of Truth into your life.

- ❖ Helps you constantly.

- ❖ Considers you special; He has become your Father, and He has given you continuous access to Him. Nobody can pay for this. Jesus has paid the price exclusively for those who come to Him and believe in Him. The world cannot receive this presence of the Holy Spirit.

It's with this understanding that we need to approach the rest of the Book of Acts. You will see how the Holy Spirit constantly guides the apostles and the Church into the Truth through supernatural experiences. Change came as a result of visions or Spirit interventions that were not expected by the apostles. Some decisions were reached on the basis of consensus, but they were only taken with the consent of God's Spirit.

For too long we have tended to view this New Testament book as a chronicle of events. It is much more than that. It reveals change of doctrine as a direct result of the Holy Spirit challenging what the disciples previously understood. It is a Holy Spirit experience that changed both understanding and practice. The changes in approach were not human ideas from a book or a new philosophy. The apostles did what the Spirit showed them to do. They trusted Him before they activated their own logic or that of others.

The teachings of Jesus both before the Cross and after His resurrection were not fully comprehended. Sometimes it was what the Spirit did that reminded the apostles what Jesus had taught. They needed the Spirit to guide them into the full meaning and implications of Jesus' teaching.

Some decisions in Acts seem to be made purely on the basis of common sense. As an example consider the appointment of the seven men to oversee the distribution of food to the widows. The process was much more than practical (see Acts 6:1-7). Notice how:

❖ The apostles laid down the spiritual criteria.

❖ The people were to decide the appointees.

❖ The apostles then confirmed the appointments.

This was the first recorded decision of this nature after Pentecost. It involved the Spirit (the appointees were required to be full of the Spirit, wisdom, etc.). Neither democracy nor autocracy (of the apostles) held sway. The people were involved. The apostles ratified the appointments after the Spirit and the people decided.

On the other hand, the apostles implemented significant doctrinal decisions as a direct result of revelation and manifestation, not human endeavor. The Spirit was indeed moving within the disciples. For example, although Jesus spent 40 days teaching the apostles about the Kingdom before He ascended into Heaven and He led and taught them for three years, when Peter and John healed the paralyzed man they were questioned by the theologians of the day—who called them *uneducated*. So the wisdom by which the disciples answered their accusers certainly did not come from a formal education. Their responses were by the Spirit and neither by quoting Scripture nor outlining their theology—they responded as a result of being in His presence.

It was their deeds, moving in the Holy Spirit's power, healing the paralyzed man that challenged the pre-conceived ideas of the day. Their acts spoke for themselves because the Spirit was speaking for Himself. There was good fruit. That is how God's servants were and how they came to be known and should be true for us as well.

The next chapter highlights Acts chapter 10 and how the Spirit of Truth fits into the fabric of our lives.

Chapter Eight

THE SPIRIT AND THE GENTILES

Chapter 10 in the Book of Acts sets out what we need to see to reach an understanding of how Truth is received and changes are made. At the opening of this chapter nothing very significant has taken place in terms of advances in doctrine; but the *events* recorded change some of the basic assumptions held by the apostles up until this time.

As mentioned previously, but worth citing again, God establishes change:

❖ Not through research or good ideas.

❖ By the working of the Holy Spirit.

❖ Still today by the Holy Spirit.

❖ Always to advance His purpose on earth.

❖ So His people can learn the Truth—through hearing Him speak to them through His Holy Spirit.

As things stand in Acts 10, the church is still essentially comprised of Jews. Those who heard the Gospel and responded were all Jews because we know they had gathered for a Jewish festival. But God was about to change the status quo. It's important to see how God establishes changes.

It would be good if the church today would allow Him to continue to bring change in the same way He did in Acts 10. I realize that for many the questioning of doctrines and practices can be very painful, or shocking. So it is easy to imagine that what was about to change for those who heard Peter would shake their understanding and practice that had continued for centuries. It wasn't any easier for them than it may be for us; but they were able to embrace Truth as it was revealed to them—even when it came through a person (unlike the Day of Pentecost). Others received the revelation as Truth and acted upon it.

This all brings up another aspect for the believer in the 21st century to consider: *Can I receive the Truth as revealed by the Spirit to one other believer (probably specifically an apostolic ministry) and apply it to my life?* My only confidence is based on the facts that I know and recognize both the gift of God in the person and I know the integrity of the person's heart. We have to be ready because revelation tends to come when we don't expect it.

In Acts 10 Peter is on a roof praying while others prepared food. Suddenly he is in a trance. He sees bizarre things. For the modern mind it could be dismissed as wild imagination—for Peter it is something very real. It is from God.

He sees a sheet lowered from Heaven and it contains animals, which were in the unclean category under the Law. A voice from Heaven (God) tells Peter to take and eat. Like all Jews, Peter knows what he is allowed to eat. When he says no the voice then tells him not to call unclean what God has cleansed. This happens three times.

To the Western mind, this is nothing out of the ordinary. For the Jew of that time it was very disturbing. All the code of laws was based on the original Ten Commandments God gave directly to Moses and the regulations God also gave him for daily life and relationship with Him. Everything that was built into their culture was based on those laws.

Peter's vision challenged everything coming from the Law of Moses. Strictly speaking this was religious dynamite. Jesus had been accused and crucified because He had operated outside the Law as the Jews perceived it.

As a result of this vision seen by Peter, everything was again put under question. The biggest dilemma for Peter was how he could explain it to the other believers. Could he expect them to believe it? What if they didn't? What would happen to him?

We cannot afford to take this vision and change lightly. Here was a potentially huge doctrinal crisis. It couldn't be handled purely on either human reasoning or the Scriptures. There had to be another way of bringing this Truth to light.

As far as we know Peter did not say anything to the others who were with him. If he did, then it is almost certain that it was not received because of the reaction of the believers later in the house of Cornelius. Perhaps he did not move in the flesh; he left things to God.

What Peter did not know was that God had been moving elsewhere at the same time. An angel appeared at the house of Cornelius and as a result of the angel's message, Cornelius sent messengers to find Peter. As Peter came down from the roof, the men sent by Cornelius were there to meet him. God was at work by His Spirit and:

- ❖ Peter had a strange vision.

- ❖ The vision was from God.

- ❖ The vision brought a fundamental change to existing doctrine.

- ❖ An angel appeared to a non-Jew.

- ❖ Details were given about Peter and the need to send for him.

- ❖ Messengers were sent.

- ❖ The messengers arrived just at the moment when Peter had received the vision.

The fundamental change in doctrine takes place as a result of a series of supernatural interventions.

So Peter goes with his companions and the messengers sent by Cornelius to his house. When he arrives there, Cornelius has gathered a number of friends to hear Peter speak. There is nothing unusual about this, after all Peter spoke on the Day of Pentecost. He had also been teaching, travelled to Samaria with John, and had seen the Holy Spirit move.

Now, in this Gentile (non-Jew) setting, Peter is sharing what he knows. He has no other objective than to fulfill the commission God gave him. But Holy Spirit-driven events overtake Peter and it's while he is speaking when the Holy Spirit comes upon the non-Jews present. There is no doubt about this. It was the Holy Spirit. The Holy Spirit fell on the people present just as He had on them *at the beginning!* They heard the Gentiles speaking in tongues. They saw they were all filled with the Holy Spirit. They had received *the Gift of the Holy Spirit* (see Acts 10:45)!

There are three things to note:

- ❖ The believers recognize that it's the working of the Holy Spirit because He has come on the Gentiles just as He did on the believers on the Day of Pentecost.

- ❖ They are shocked by the event because God is dealing with Gentile and Jew alike.

- ❖ The challenge to their belief system comes through the Spirit entirely.

- ❖ It is the manifestation of the Holy Spirit that establishes new Truth for the Jewish believers.

This entire experience was a sharp challenge from God, by the presence and actions of the Holy Spirit, to the presumptions of the Jewish believers of the day. Some may already have spent three years with Jesus (at least Peter had) and noticed how His life, teachings, and actions challenged the traditions and assumptions of His day. This move of the Holy Spirit went well beyond the days of Jesus' earthly ministry. It was true that He had brought both blessing and healing to non-Jews. However, it was this manifestation of the Spirit on the Gentiles that sealed them with the identity of God. God's people were no longer an exclusive nation of Jews. Gentiles had become believers, were received by God, and were supernaturally endowed with His Spirit.

God made a change through the Holy Spirit—there was no theological debate. What took place in the house of Cornelius was by the power of

God and based on the revelation Peter had previously received. What challenges all of us is that this intervention by the Holy Spirit went beyond the manifestations of God's power during Jesus' earthly life. It also took the Gospel message beyond the Jewish cultural and religious setting into the Gentile world. The Holy Spirit was expanding on and developing the original Truth embodied in Jesus and expressed in His life. This still happens today.

During the 40 days Jesus taught the disciples after His resurrection, He apparently did not prepare them for everything God had planned. If Jesus had told them about the coming of the Spirit to the Gentiles they wouldn't have felt so challenged about what happened at Cornelius' house. Jesus had not told them about it before His ascension into Heaven. They had to learn from the Spirit through His manifestation and their experience of Him.

So Acts chapter 10 shows us that doctrine was not established by the Scriptures alone, but by the revelation and the move of the Spirit. Truth developed and extended beyond previous experiences and assumptions.

Although Old Testament passages and the life of Jesus at least hinted that the Gospel would be for all people in all nations, this Truth was not established until the Holy Spirit moved. Today He is still moving, still extending and stretching our understanding and application of Scripture. We need the Spirit of God to continue to guide us into all the Truth, expanding our experience by revelation.

Chapter Nine

THE TRUTH AND PAUL

Of all the characters in the New Testament, I think Saul turned Paul is one of the most exciting as well as significant. His importance may be summarized as follows:

- ❖ He was the most prolific writer of all the New Testament authors.

- ❖ He had strong theological and training roots within Judaism.

- ❖ His transformation from persecutor to pioneer is mind-blowing.

- ❖ In spite of his Jewish culture he went into the Gentile world to fulfill his gift and call.

- ❖ His apostolic ministry is significant in terms of:

  - ‣ The amount of Scripture he wrote in the New Testament.

  - ‣ His unique call at that time to the Gentiles.

  - ‣ His success in sharing the Gospel.

  - ‣ His influence theologically.

❖ The theology outlined in his Epistles has over the centuries been the basis of New Testament scholarship from his time unto present day.

❖ His apostolic journeys and faith exploits form most of the apostle's work contained in the Book of Acts.

Background

Paul was steeped in knowledge of the Old Testament Scriptures. In the Bible he describes himself as a Hebrew of the Hebrews. He was taught by Gamaliel—one of the best teachers of the Jewish faith in his day. If anyone could have found out purely from the Old Testament that Jesus was indeed the Messiah, it was surely Paul. He had a keen understanding of the prophets who foretold the coming of Jesus, yet he failed to recognize Him.

This is essential to our understanding of the New Testament. Paul's importance as a teacher, scholar, and theologian was surpassed by something else, which actually brought him to Christ. It was certainly not the Scriptures. He knew no more Scripture immediately after his conversion experience than he did before. What took place was beyond intelligence, understanding, and natural explanation. It was supernatural. It speaks of a spiritual experience. This kind of encounter with God through the activity of the Holy Spirit is still the requirement for entry into true sonship in Jesus Christ today.

> For you have not received a spirit of slavery leading to fear again, but you have received a spirit of adoption as sons by which we cry out, "Abba! Father!" The Spirit Himself bears witness with our spirit that we are children of God (Romans 8:15-16).

All Paul's training and education had no explanation either for or against his encounter with Jesus on the Damascus road. His friends were helpless. In a few moments, Saul turned from being a leader of persecutors of the Church to Paul, a submissive follower of Jesus. He had a Spirit encounter that brought change to his direction and destiny. Understanding the importance of the Holy Spirit in the lives of believers in New Testament times brings us closer to the Truth.

The Truth and Paul

SAUL THE PERSECUTOR, PAUL THE PROCLAIMER

It was Paul's own admittance that he had a zeal for God. This enthusiasm caused him to persecute the Church of Jesus. His zeal for God actually blinded him to the revelation of Jesus. He was so convinced of the truth he had received that he missed when it appeared in the form of a man (Jesus). He ran with the revelation passed on to him by those who taught him. As he proclaimed this teaching, he failed to see the new. Dare I say *we too can be like that?* Church history tells me we can. As I look back over my own history I see times of opposition to:

❖ New birth.

❖ Baptism in the Spirit and speaking in tongues.

❖ Dance (and other things) acceptable to God in worship.

❖ Any manifestation of the Spirit that could not be understood with the mind or beyond my own experience (what this book is about!).

❖ Things foreign to my own culture.

The list is longer; however, I must admit that many of my attitudes stemmed from a fear of what I did not know in my own experience, and the fear of bringing division. These attitudes resulted in my need to control people, especially when I became a church leader. Leaders act and react, today and in Paul's time, out of a variety of motivations—when they allow the Holy Spirit to guide them, only then are the change appropriate and real.

Saul's persecution of the Church was typified in Luke's account of the martyrdom of Stephen (Acts 7:59-8:1). As far as we know, Stephen was the first to die for his faith in Jesus. If this is indeed the case, it again highlights the special place of Saul in the life of the early Church. He was directly responsible for the death of the first martyr, but he later found the grace of God. Stephen was a good man, appointed because of his faith, character, and experience of the Spirit to oversee the distribution of food to widows. As he died, people saw that his face was like the face of an angel. Only a callous, religious fanatic could have wanted to murder him so brutally. Paul was such a man.

It is very significant that Luke comments how Paul *consented* to Stephen's death. It's as though his opinion was important. The context is just after Stephen has appealed to God for forgiveness for those who are killing him. Let's be real. Naturally speaking Saul would not have been our first choice of someone who would become a faithful follower of Jesus! In fact, after his conversion the disciples were not keen to accept him. This is another example of how we, leaders or not, let history hinder us from accepting the changes and advancements that come by the Spirit. Saul the persecutor became Paul the proclaimer—great in the Kingdom of God. Our past mistakes do not have to hold us back no matter how terrible they may have been. We should also make sure that we don't hold the past errors of others against their future success if they, like us, have been through genuine repentance—like Paul.

Grace element is evident here. Paul had not merited the intervention, which took place on the Damascus road. Far from it! Grace is beyond our human understanding. When Paul later explained the grace of God to other believers, he wrote from experience, not just concepts. Perhaps this is the case with all the writers of the New Testament. The truth they wrote was what they experienced. I could write an entire book on this subject!

Another note about Paul. Paul's own testimony of his conversion experience (see Acts 26) sheds further light on how he came to Christ. In this passage Paul talks to King Agrippa and quotes the words of Jesus, *"It is hard for you to kick against the goads."* I am sure that this is talking about the convicting presence of the Holy Spirit. It ties in with the over-wrought zeal displayed by Saul toward the followers of Jesus—a reaction to the Truth. It seems that he may have known what God wanted all along and in the end became one of God's reluctant leaders!

To summarize, Saul, before his conversion and as a persecutor of the Church, had:

❖ A totally misguided zeal.

❖ The Holy Spirit convicting him.

❖ To experience God's grace.

❖ His previous experiences as a foundation for his theology and his ministry as an apostle.

Paul wrote about grace so effectively because he received and experienced it personally. Experience gives us the right to pass on to others. The same is borne out in the writings of John.

THE ROAD TO DAMASCUS

In Acts 9, the beginning of the chapter concerning Saul's (Paul) conversion shows that he had official permission from the high priest in Jerusalem to go to Damascus to slaughter the believers there. One moment he was an ambassador on behalf of the high priest and the next an ambassador for Jesus. God can take what we are, transform it, and yet retain aspects of our history. Paul changed in character, charisma, and calling; yet he remained a zealot for God, an ambassador, and a teacher. So, although Paul's orientation changed, he is still recognized as the same man.

Earlier in life when I was teaching, I pioneered a department in a high school. I entered fully into the life of the school and participated in sports and French outside school hours. I did not seek a comfortable life. Because of my full schedule, when the time came, it was easy to adjust or transform into full-time ministry (though we are already full-time…or we should be!) without much difficulty. I already operated on the basis that my life was God's. So, although my orientation changed, I was still recognized as the same man.

In a day when so many spend their lives selfishly safeguarding and trying to extend their own rights, God's people can still work for His rights and carry His heart into the world. In other words, we should be ambassadors ready to extend and expand His Kingdom, not our own selfish aims—or ministry!

In chapter one of his book, *What Shall this Man Do?* Watchman Nee points to this orientation adjustment with Jesus' disciples. Peter was always fishing, walking on water, or just doing something! John was in the boat with his father mending nets. John's writings speak of the same things in a spiritual setting with his focus on love, relationship, and unity. John and Peter were fishermen with different personalities, but they were on the same Holy Spirit mission to expand His Kingdom!

Saul's committed intention to go to Damascus and destroy the followers of Jesus there was interrupted by a *suddenly* of God. He was carrying all the credentials he needed to act against the believers and take them bound to Jerusalem. Everything was going fine; but a *suddenly* from God changed everything—his purpose and direction for life. As he was on the road a light shone down from Heaven.

Some modern theologians tend not to like this kind of passage because it goes beyond rational thinking. Outside the Holy Spirit it makes no sense at all. A light flashed from heaven. A voice was heard. Saul's travelling companions also heard the voice but could see no one. They were witnesses—nobody could question his experience of the Holy Spirit. He fell to the ground under the power of God.

This was no empty manifestation. Why am I so confident? Because the man who got up from the ground was different from the one who fell down. He encountered God. None of his teaching or knowledge had ever given him this experience. It was beyond human explanation. It's great to see people fall to the ground when coming under the power of the Spirit. Can I say again that when Saul fell to the ground, he was different when he got up! Something happened. Manifestations like that should always bring change—for us too. So often we seem to fail to allow the Holy Spirit to complete what He wants to do.

As the voice spoke to him, a change of authority took place in Saul. The paper credentials he carried with him were counted as nothing as the voice gave him clear direction. The voice rebuked Saul for his persecution of Jesus. This must have been astonishing to his travelling companions. He had authority from the chief priest—the highest spiritual authority in Israel. Who could override him?

The authority at work here is from Heaven. It cuts through human order because it is from God. It takes the man and confronts him with the Spirit. As members of God's Church we need to note this and live appropriately when God's sovereignty causes Him to move in such a profound way.

THE COMPANIONS

What happened to Saul along the road had an effect on his companions as well. Saul heard the voice that spoke to him and was also blinded. His companions also heard the voice but could not see where it came from. We can assume that because they were travelling with him they were probably in general agreement with Saul in his understanding of Jesus and his intention to bind those of "The Way" and take them captive to Jerusalem. The intriguing thing is that those same like-minded friends must have taken him on to Damascus after the suddenly. Why would they do this if he was now professing Christ unless they too had been affected?

I believe this is something important to understand. When God intervenes, when the Holy Spirit moves in power, that moving affects, or should affect, more than just the individual concerned. We see that this is the case countless times in the Gospels. Jesus, before ascending into Heaven, tells His disciples that they are also to move in power when the Holy Spirit comes on them to be His witnesses (see Acts 1:8). As Acts unfolds, the original disciples and others do move in power. Paul is one of the many other believers who move in the power of the Holy Spirit.

The subject of the power of the Holy Spirit as an essential part of the presentation of the Gospel in the New Testament could be the focus of a lengthy study. The moving of the Holy Spirit in a situation or circumstance has caused whole gatherings of people to become believers; so it follows that a life changed by the power of God causes others to be touched as well.

We see that the encounter on the road to Damascus brought sudden transformation to one man and it also touched his fellow travellers. All this took place because of the supernatural moving of God. Saul was already a man of the Word. He was then transferred into a supernatural realm. This happens not only to him on the road—there is more for him to experience after he arrived in Damascus. This is also true for all of us. God takes us on to visions and revelations. As believers we are all called to move in His power (see Mark 16:17-18).

DAMASCUS

Revelation continues at a pace when Paul reaches Damascus. Two things seem to happen simultaneously. Perhaps we tend to forget the many ways God works to bring things together so His plans are realized.

First, a disciple of Jesus named Ananias receives a revelation. In a vision Jesus speaks to him and is told:

❖ Go to a street called Straight.

❖ Ask for the house of Judas.

❖ Inquire for Saul who is from Tarsus.

Second, Paul is praying and:

❖ He sees a vision.

❖ He is told that a man called Ananias will come and lay hands on him.

❖ He will receive his sight.

These visions and revelations are wholly supernatural—a bit like in Acts 10 with Peter and Cornelius. The Lord reveals Himself to both men. He gives them parallel information to which they are to respond. When we consider Paul and Ananias, we note that the supernatural event on the Damascus road is not in isolation. More revelation is required.

The current revelation of Jesus we have come to know may not be enough—God is ready to move in further revelation than what we have already received. He is very likely to use others in bringing further revelation than just using one specific ministry. We cannot be so arrogant as to believe that we don't need more revelation or the revelation God might bring through others. I believe people are experiencing ongoing revelation from God as He unveils more of His purposes to and in His people at large.

One of the amazing things about the passage in Acts chapter 9 is that Ananias actually does what Jesus tells him supernaturally to do. Saul had been threatening the lives of God's people in Damascus—including that of Ananias himself! So Ananias has to go through his own faith crisis and actually go and ask for Saul of Tarsus—the persecutor. God has clearly spoken but faith has to engage beyond the normal. For all of us this kind of event can be a struggle. God wants us to be ready to trust Him as He stretches us in our experience. For Ananias what was asked of him was not comfortable, easy, or safe.

It is the vision, the revelation that produces an increase in faith-experience and trust of God. Without supernatural intervention Ananias would never have gone to Saul. Saul would never have received his sight. Paul would not have been able to do all that God wanted him to do. We must always be open to intervention of a supernatural order if we are to do all that God wants of us.

When we become involved with God at this level (and it can happen to anyone!), we reach the point where we cannot go back. It's impossible. We are more than caught up in the Spirit. We are fused to the power and will of God in a oneness with Him similar to that of Jesus with His Father as He went to Gethsemane. This is in line with what Jesus prayed for us in John 17:20-23 (KJV) "... *That they all may be one; as thou, Father, art in me, and I in thee...*" The purpose is great and God's method of delivery through the Holy Spirit tends to be people, including you and me.

Sometimes it is difficult for us to follow through with what God speaks because we think we will look or sound stupid or odd if we do what He says. We may even think it really wasn't God speaking. So we have to learn to recognize when it is God by being obedient. If we do nothing because it doesn't make sense, then we prevent ourselves from hearing God. If Peter could make so many mistakes while trying to do what was right, then we can too. At the very least we can learn from the times we get it wrong!

When I was a student, some of us were chosen to distribute leaflets announcing an evangelistic event. The idea of knocking on students' doors and inviting them terrified me! So instead I just pushed the leaflets under doors and went rapidly back to the room where we were meeting, "so I could pray for the others"! A real spiritual...*coward.*

As I sat there, God started to impress on me I should go to the room of a girl student I knew. I was so convinced of this I ran through the corridors to her room. When I arrived at her door I suddenly felt stupid. *What if...?*

Eventually I tapped on her door, and heard her say, "Come in." As I pushed the door open, I saw a room full of students. They were sitting everywhere—on the bed, the floor, on chairs. I felt so embarrassed that I just stood there. "Are you coming in?" the girl asked. I replied, "No," but then added that the reason I was there seemed so silly. I told her I thought God wanted me to go to her room. Everyone in the room broke out into fits of laughter. Only one guy wasn't laughing, and they were all looking at him.

Apparently before I knocked on the door, one of the evangelistic event leaflets had been pushed under the door. There was some discussion about it and one particular young man said, "If God really exists then He's going to have to prove it to me." Right then came my knock at the door. I was overwhelmed. The guy was overwhelmed—and became born again. Of course he did! He had experienced the supernatural. Jesus was not ashamed of moving in the power of the Spirit. Nor should we be. Trust God in every thing.

I have to say that even since those days I have had a lot to learn—and am still learning! For years, I did not always follow through on what God spoke to me. However inadequate I felt, God used me anyway. He still does.

God uses the supernatural (revelation, angelic visitation, and prophecy) to establish His truth in the lives of His people. This is true when we are born again. It is as true for us today as it was in the Book of Acts. Nothing has changed—nor has God.

ANANIAS

So Ananias goes through a challenging process to achieve what God is asking of him. Can you imagine how he feels as he approaches the street called Straight? Then he finds out there is a man called Simon the Tanner who lives there.

God could also have told him in which house Simon lived. So why didn't He? I believe we see a grace process, which helps us understand God's gentleness as He takes us forward into the supernatural. God takes Ananias (and us) forward step by step. As we obey in a little, we are encouraged to go further into the things God says to us. As Ananias hears that Simon lives on that street, he has to be encouraged that he heard God correctly and that everything else He said will be right. God deliberately omitted a portion so Simon will learn to trust God for the rest of his mission. If he had known all the details, he would never have had to ask for directions to the house.

Ananias must have approached the house with a sense of excitement, perhaps tinged with uncertainty because it was the first time God had spoken to him in this way. It was certainly the most risky thing he had been asked to do. Let's be real—this is how faith operates. We follow, do as God says, grow in faith as we see God more, and then gain confidence to trust Him more and in a bigger way.

THE MINISTRY OF ANANIAS

No further reference is made to this man, Ananias, throughout the remainder of the New Testament. His contribution in terms of what is written in the Book of Acts is minimal. The consequences are huge!

As Ananias lays his hands on Paul, who is destined for greatness, he sees him filled with the Spirit and Paul's sight is restored. God has moved powerfully through a common person to bring release who one who will have profound and eternal effects in spreading the Gospel through his travels, establishing churches around the Eastern Mediterranean regions, and in laying down a broad theological foundation for the Church at large through his writings.

The ordinary one releases the great one—similar to John the Baptist bringing release to Jesus' ministry by baptizing Him. Jesus needed to be baptized by John to go on to greater ministry. Submission and humility are key characteristics of the man or woman of God who would be like Jesus. Paul needed Ananias to pray for him so he could be filled with the Spirit, have his sight restored, and be released to a greater ministry.

God wants you and me. However ordinary we may be, to move in the supernatural. It takes and helps go people further into the Truth and their experience of it. You may feel common or insignificant. So were Ananias and John the Baptist—but how God used them when they followed through with what God wanted!

In the early days when I was a member of a church, which moved in the Spirit, I met two very significant women. One was the wife of a retired coal miner. God revealed things to this woman in the most amazing ways. She saw things in depth. She moved powerfully in words of knowledge. She was also a tremendous help to me in those days when I discovering more about the Holy Spirit.

The second woman was totally different. She carried wisdom in the Spirit, which I had never encountered before. She had the ability to take a prayer meeting from death to life in one sentence. She was powerful; but she was also very ordinary.

Both women may have been *ordinary* but what made them *extraordinary* was their obedience to receive the supernatural Spirit of Truth. God communicates Truth by the Spirit through people who seem *ordinary*. Ananias moved in miracle power toward Saul of Tarsus. Even if Saul felt he could not fulfill God's commission to him, he became more and more aware of the supernatural power of God. His gateway into God's purpose for his life was entirely beyond his theological experience and understanding. He had to leave that behind in order to enter into a new truth about God based on the powerful Spirit of Truth rather than on his previous legalistic adherence to the Old Testament Scriptures.

When the persecutor Saul of Tarsus encountered the light shining on the road to Damascus, it was clear evidence that the darkness in his life was confronted by the Light. Blinded, he was set apart from his friends, he became isolated. You see we cannot just look at what is good. Whenever anyone comes to God there are difficulties to face as well as blessings to enjoy. We want to make it easy for people. God doesn't. He wants to establish a faith walk in each of us.

A while ago I heard a report concerning the increase of asthma as a disease among young people. Asthma has been around for a long time. I recall a school friend who was crippled with the illness and died as a result of it at the age of 14. However, now there is a massive increase in asthma particularly among young people. The report strongly suggested that one of the key reasons for the rise in asthma cases might be a direct result of over protection of young children from harmful bacteria. It was suggested that the lack of bacteria exposure prevented their bodies from establishing an effective immune system. This made me think of my grandmother saying, "a little bit of dirt never did anyone any harm."

It's the same with faith. God has brought us to a *living* faith. But in several places in the New Testament there is a strong emphasis on the need for faith to grow. If it doesn't face issues, it will never grow. Difficulties, crises, can be God's means to equip us, enlarge our faith, mature and strengthen us. If we constantly engage with the Holy Spirit, this will happen every time situations arise for us. In other words, this is how the Truth develops in us—experiencing God through the Holy Spirit and moving in faith and obedience in response to Him.

The initial challenges that new converts face are the reasons why the Bible talks of milk rather than meat needed to sustain them.

Notice these verses:

And I, brethren, could not speak to you as to spiritual men, but as to men of flesh, as to babes in Christ. I gave you milk to drink, not solid food for you were not yet able to receive it. Indeed, even now you are not yet able, for you are still fleshly. For since there is jealousy and strife among you, are you not fleshly...(1 Corinthians 3:1-3).

Paul is saying that new believers haven't grown up in their faith yet. Their faith has not been tried, so they have not become strong.

For instance, a mother will not deliberately keep feeding a child milk if she wants her baby to grow properly. The child's bones and teeth will not become strong. Nor would she want to keep her little one in diapers. The child matures in different stages and ages depending on circumstances and experiences. It's the same for the Christian. Paul went through trials as a young believer but grew quickly as a result. Faith is essential to Paul in his ministry life. Ananias' input into Paul's life took him further into the world of supernatural faith life.

Chapter Ten

PAUL AND BARNABAS

Much is written in the Book of Acts about Paul's ministry as it matures and expands. *Separation* is a strong theme at the beginning of Acts 13 when Barnabas and Paul were *separated* to the work to which they were called. It was not separation *from* the rest. They remained in ministry, with Antioch as the base church. The separation of Barnabas and Paul in Acts 15 can be seen not as division but as multiplication. Paul was separated *to* Silas. Barnabas was separated *to* Mark. Thus the work of God grew; it did not suffer.

The subject of separation and the Truth is dealt with in a later chapter. For the moment, let's recognize that the Truth does separate. When anyone becomes born again, the Truth enters them. In spiritual terms they are immediately separated from unbelief and ungodliness to the family of God.

Barnabas' first appearance in the Book of Acts defines his life. He is named a son of encouragement (see Acts 4:36). Hopefully, many of us will be encouraged in ourselves to note that one as great as Paul would need someone to encourage him! Like us, Barnabas seems to be a very ordinary kind of man. However, the relatively small inclusion of him in Acts carries significance.

Before Paul's conversion, he was isolated from the Church because of his history of violence against the Christians. Perhaps it is encouraging to note that:

- ❖ You are not the first to feel isolated in the community of the Church as a result of: your history, your encounter with God, or other believers struggling to accept you as part of God's Church.

- ❖ Those who have been believers for a long time can actually be fearful of a new convert.

- ❖ The early church was not perfect. In the matter of Paul's conversion there was a lack of faith and that lack limited them in their love.

It is into this context that an ordinary man called Barnabas comes. Note this passage from Acts 9:26-31:

> And when he had come to Jerusalem, he was trying to associate with the disciples; and they were all afraid of him, not believing that he was a disciple. But Barnabas took hold of him and brought him to the apostles and described to them how he had seen the Lord on the road, and that He had talked to him, and how at Damascus he had spoken out boldly in the name of Jesus. And he was with them moving about freely in Jerusalem, speaking out boldly in the name of the Lord. And he was talking and arguing with the Hellenistic Jews; but they were attempting to put him to death. But when the brethren learned of it, they brought him down to Caesarea and sent him away to Tarsus. So the church throughout all Judea and Galilee and Samaria enjoyed peace, being built up; and, going on in the fear of the Lord and in the comfort of the Holy Spirit, it continued to increase.

Sometimes believers really are like sheep! We congregate together. How good it is that Barnabas had his own faith for the call of God on his life and was an ordinary but fearless man. He would stand in the gap. His faith shone out against:

- ❖ The persecutors of the church.

❖ The fearful believers living at Jerusalem, the place of the apostolic seat for the church.

❖ The skepticism about the reality of Paul's conversion experience.

❖ The example of other believers who should have known better.

Yet Barnabas was an ordinary man—like you and me; but he could do what God was asking of him. So can we through the power of the Spirit of Truth. The earth has a countless resource of ordinary believers who will be called on in faith to take action. If our time hasn't yet come, it will. In fact we may be called of God several times throughout our lifetime to stand in the gap. This is one way in which we live and sow the Truth.

Too often godly leadership stands against the majority only to find the weight of democratic argument and debate drowns out the lone voice of faith truth. When the time comes, be the Barnabas who liberates the apostle.

Much might not have been achieved in the spread of the Gospel if Barnabas had not taken Paul under his care. That was all he did; but he was instrumental in releasing one of the greatest men who ever proclaimed Jesus.

Although he stood alone, Barnabas was prepared to run with the revelation of who Paul was and was to become. In this he embraced the truth he knew of Paul and acted upon it without the fear of potential consequences. To work the works of God, to walk in His Truth, we can and should also act on the revelation that comes by the Spirit of Truth.

ANTIOCH

Barnabas was sent from the church in Jerusalem to the church at Antioch. The Bible is clear that when he saw the grace of God, he went for Paul to take him there with him (see Acts 11:22-24). Barnabas so believed in the call of God on Paul that he acts on the revelation, because revelation is Truth.

Both stay in Antioch for some time and are recognized in the ministry as either prophets or teachers. Then the Holy Spirit reveals their ultimate call as apostles. In Acts 13 a prophetic utterance calls all the men of ministry in the church at Antioch to release both men to their apostolic call. Thus they depart on what should be known as Paul's first apostolic journey. Barnabas was courageous in bringing about this release for Paul. They depart as Barnabas and Paul; they quickly become Paul and Barnabas.

So Paul takes the ascendancy. He increasingly becomes the most influential apostolic figure in the New Testament. From this point his deeds, writings, and theology will be the most significant of all New Testament writers. There is a progressive process in which the teacher becomes the accomplished apostle.

Part Four

New Testament Writers

INTRODUCTION

Part Four examines New Testament writings to see how they blend with the teachings of Jesus and Luke's Book of Acts. You will notice how the New Testament interprets the Old, and how there is a oneness throughout New Covenant writings confirming unity in life, Truth, and Spirit. There is also a replacement to Law as set out in the Old Testament.

There are passages in the New Testament that reveal how inspired the writers are. It was not so much that they took the literal view of things expressed in the Old Testament; rather they interpreted them in the light of the New Covenant established through the life and death of Jesus. In some cases, the Scripture was interpreted in such a way as to fit the context of the experience lived by the early believers.

Chapter Eleven

Matthew's Gospel

Interpretation of the Old Testament

Matthew is a Jew. That is why he is able (more than Luke, for example) to bring his own cross-reference between the Old Testament and his own writings.

In the early chapter of Matthew's Gospel, there are references to Old Testament passages. Several of these occur about the time of the birth of Jesus. Let's examine some of these passages:

> Now all this took place that what was spoken by the Lord through the prophet might be fulfilled, saying, "BEHOLD, THE VIRGIN SHALL BE WITH CHILD, AND SHALL BEAR A SON, AND THEY SHALL CALL HIS NAME IMMANUEL," which translated means, "GOD WITH US" (Matthew 1:22-23).

This is a well-known passage. At Christmas time it is one of the most memorable and tends to be read in Christian gatherings. Matthew, in the New Testament, clearly applies it to the birth of Jesus. Matthew writes that Isaiah's prophecy in the Old Testament was fulfilled. (See Isaiah 7:14.)

Matthew goes beyond the literalist interpretation of the original passage and its context. He applies it directly to Jesus. It was not necessary for him to do that but I believe he did so to give evidence to his Hebrew readers that the details of the birth of Jesus were found in the Old Testament. In this way he verified the birth of the Messiah to the Jewish people.

> And they said to him, "In Bethlehem of Judea, for so it has been written by the prophet, 'AND YOU, BETHLEHEM, LAND OF JUDAH, ARE BY NO MEANS LEAST AMONG THE LEADERS OF JUDAH; FOR OUT OF YOU SHALL COME FORTH A RULER, WHO WILL SHEPHERD MY PEOPLE ISRAEL'" (Matthew 2:5-6).

> And he arose and took the Child and His mother by night, and departed for Egypt; and was there until the death of Herod, that what was spoken by the Lord through the prophet might be fulfilled, saying, "OUT OF EGYPT DID I CALL MY SON" (Matthew 2:14-15).

These New Testament passages have a similar meaning. The original passage is found in the Old Testament—Hosea 11:1, "When Israel was a child, then I loved him, and called my son out of Egypt." The direct context is entirely that of God calling His people out of Egypt through Moses. This is clear because Hosea further says in the same chapter "the more I called Israel, the further they went from me." So Matthew takes a small phrase out of a passage connected with the captivity in Egypt and makes it fit the New Testament context of the birth of Jesus.

The argument for such a Scripture link is weak unless we understand that Matthew was writing under the inspiration of the Holy Spirit. The Spirit was guiding him into the Truth. If Matthew was able to interpret Scripture accurately and differently by the Spirit, then so should the people of God today. We cannot confine the Spirit of God to our current interpretation of the Book He wrote!

I realize that this is a contentious issue; but in the end we have to trust the Holy Spirit. If we fail to trust Him, then we do not allow Him to continue to guide us into all Truth. I am not speaking for the blatant contradiction of Scripture; I am speaking against a theology that does not allow further interpretation of the Scriptures to us by the Holy Spirit, the One who inspired them! Thank God for His gifted people who take us further into the revelation of the Scriptures. It must continue so we increase in our awareness and experience of the Truth by the Spirit.

> Then that which was spoken through Jeremiah the prophet was fulfilled, say-ing, "A VOICE WAS HEARD IN RAMAH, WEEPING AND GREAT MOURNING, RACHEL WEEPING FOR HER CHIL-DREN; AND SHE REFUSED TO BE COMFORTED, BECAUSE THEY WERE NO MORE" (Matthew 2:17-18).

Similar things can be said of this passage. A cursory look at Jeremiah 31:15, *"Thus says the LORD, A voice is heard in Ramah, Lamentation and bitter weep-ing Rachel is weeping for her children; She refuses to be comforted for her children, Be-cause they are no more"* is sufficient evidence that the immediate context has nothing to do with the coming of the Messiah. Yet, again, we accept the in-spiration of the Holy Spirit bringing fresh revelation to Matthew as he writes about Jesus.

Over 30 years ago I was invited by the local church leader to be leader with him of a church house party. He was clearly in charge and gave me just one short session to speak over the days we spent there. Although I was a leader in title, I was not in terms of what took place.

For my session I spoke about a parable in Luke and expounded on the work of the Holy Spirit. When I finished he slated me, restricting the Truth to the immediate context of Jewish culture. I was totally gutted. I felt everything I said was right; he had said otherwise. Later the leader's wife (he had a diploma; she had a graduate degree in theology) told me what I said was excellent and that she got a lot out of it. Her husband was never confronted by either of us. Sadly, his narrow view of Scripture and its interpretation left me in bondage for years.

You may have encountered a similar situation—that is why we need to understand the Holy Spirit and the Truth. God has more to say. We cannot restrict the Holy Spirit in His interpretation of the Scriptures. We do need to guard against heresy, however. But we should be open in Spirit just as the early believers were in the house of Cornelius. We have no immediate doctrinal basis for believing that we should be different than them.

There are a few other passages quoted by Matthew from the Old Tes-tament. Perhaps I should emphasize again that there are many more references in his Gospel to the Old Testament and most of them would not have the kind of interpretation given to those quoted previously. What I want to highlight is that there are valid exceptions to the usual ways of interpretation.

For further study read these Scripture passages in Matthew: 2:22; 3:3; 4:4-16; 8:16-17; 12:15-21; 12:39; 13:13-15; 13:34-35; 15:7-9; 21:4; 21:13; 21:15-16.

Satan and the Use of Scripture

At the beginning of Jesus' ministry, He is led into the wilderness and tempted by the devil. It's interesting to note that in Luke's Gospel there is a marked difference between the Jesus who entered the wilderness and the One who exited. The Bible tells us that Jesus went into the wilderness *full of the Holy Spirit and was led around by the Spirit* (Luke 4:1). After the temptations, He *returned to Galilee in the power of the Spirit* (Luke 4:14). Jesus' encounter with the devil did not hinder His fulfilling of His Father's purpose. The time of temptation actually strengthened Him in the Spirit.

Believers often fail to understand this Truth for their own lives. Jesus has won the victory. Satan, in all the evil that he does, really only gives us opportunities to win and to grow in the things of the Spirit. God causes all things to work together for our good—that includes temptation. Therefore, when we establish our lives on a clear understanding of the Father's heart, satan is no more than a tool in God's hands. It is important we embrace this fact before looking at the temptations of Jesus. The experience of His Father's heart was the basis on which Jesus was *led around by the Spirit;* a Spirit encounter took place between the forces of evil and the power of God.

The first temptation of Jesus concerns His natural needs. After 40 days of fasting, He is hungry and the devil tries to attack Him through His flesh: *"If You are the Son of God, command that these stones become bread"* (Matt. 4:3). Obviously Jesus could do that. He had the ability. In Himself, He had the right. Where He did not have the right was in His relationship with His Father. He was on earth to do the Father's will. It was not His will that Jesus turn stones into bread.

Jesus' reply: *"It is written, 'MAN SHALL NOT LIVE ON BREAD ALONE, BUT ON EVERY WORD THAT PROCEEDS OUT OF THE MOUTH OF GOD'"* was more than the throwing of a verse into the conversation (see

Matt. 4:4). This was part of His call, His ministry. His meat and drink were to do the will of the Father. He had food to eat of that others did not understand or experience. The fact that they did not have that experience did not deny the Truth of it. Since it was beyond their experience, it was also beyond their full understanding. The full Truth comes to us when we experience it. If Jesus was not living it, there would have been no point in quoting the verse to satan! Scripture has no power where it is not lived from the heart. So satan could not accuse Jesus on this or undermine Him.

When we learn to live by the Spirit, operating from the Word in our hearts and lived out in our lives, we too can handle the enemy in the same way. Scripture is powerless unless it is experienced and lived out in our daily lives from the heart.

Both the first and second temptations begin *"If you are the Son of God..."*. Satan wants Jesus to prove who He is. This is a significant aspect of the life of Jesus: He never tried to prove who He was. It was by revelation from the Father that Peter could say: *"You are the Christ, the Son of the living God."* Jesus could have told him who He was, but He didn't. He does not have to prove His existence to those who do not seek Him as Savior and Lord. That is why the experience of God is always preceded by faith in Him and who He is. We can be tempted in the same way. Satan loves to try to undermine who we are in Christ by pointing to our failings. We tend to feel we have something to prove to him. If we have nothing to prove to God we definitely don't have to with the enemy! We are what we are by the grace of God, not our own perfection.

When I was a student I had a friend who wanted to find God. He was very philosophical in his ways, and I had what seemed to be endless debates with him. Increasingly I recognized how pointless it was; he loved to debate intellectually (I quite liked it too!). One day he came to see me in the library, ready to talk. I was very brief with him and told him, *"If you want to know God then look for Him."* I ended the conversation abruptly.

Two days later I saw two or three people who all asked if I had seen Ron lately. Eventually we caught up with one another. He was elated. *"I've found God!"* he said. He explained he was just wandering by a lake and God's presence hit him. He was seeking God for who He is. He found Him. Since then He has served God in church leadership. We need to know who we are looking for and then seek Him as He is—then God is in charge of our relationship with Him from the beginning.

In the second temptation, satan actually quotes the Bible: *"If You are the Son of God throw Yourself down; for it is written, 'HE WILL GIVE HIS AN-GELS CHARGE CONCERNING YOU'; and 'ON their HANDS THEY WILL BEAR YOU UP, LEST YOU STRIKE YOUR FOOT AGAINST A STONE'"* (Matt. 4:6). I remember as a young believer struggling with this one. Satan quoted Scripture and yet Jesus did not *fulfill* what was written. It didn't seem to make sense. Why should He not do something to establish the Truth of Scripture? What was wrong with that? I lived like that for years, never understanding; just trusting that somehow Jesus knew what He was doing.

The answer is so simple. It has to do with the will of God. Whatever satan asks us to do, it will never be God's will to do it. That's why Jesus replied: *"On the other hand, it is written, 'YOU SHALL NOT PUT THE LORD YOUR GOD TO THE TEST.'"* (Matt.4:7). Any attempt to prove the Truth of God on a purely external basis (other than what the Spirit is saying within) will fail. That's why I failed so much as a new believer. The external, written Word of God, well taught and preached, did not in itself bring the reality of Truth to my heart or into my life. I must have tempted God several times like this, always wondering why the things I looked for never seemed to happen. Academic acceptance of Truth is inadequate. Truth has to operate from the heart. It's in our hearts we come to obedience to the Father's will by the prompting of the Spirit; then we enter the realm of the miraculous.

There is much to be said about the third temptation. First of all, satan shows Jesus what he can (in the immediate) give Him. That sounds bizarre! In Eden, satan stole the hearts of God's created people. The Fall of Adam and Eve caused the whole of creation to groan. Satan became the god of this world. Through the Fall, he sought to usurp God's authority and power. In that same way he tried to get Jesus to submit to his power. He diverts worship from the only One that has the right to receive it.

As he invites Jesus to worship him, he seeks to supplant the Father in Jesus' life. We need to thank God it didn't happen! Jesus only operates in relationship with His Father. We will defeat the enemy as long as we can follow Jesus' example. We cooperate with the Spirit within us. Satan called for Jesus to *worship* him. Worship is from the heart, the seat of Truth (see John 4:22-24) because worship is loved based. With the Father at the center of our lives, we continuously experience His presence and love through the Spirit who lives in us. When we live in this way, we are much less likely to submit to satanic temptation and our own ambition.

In the third temptation, satan offers Jesus a shortcut to glory. We need to be careful about ways that boast a fast-forward into "destiny." Adam and Eve were offered a shortcut to knowledge and look what happened to them! Wherever we are in God today, it is our obligation to Him to wait for the fullness of time. That's what Jesus did (see Gal. 4:4). How badly do you want and seek your own success? Is it possible you are following satan's evil ways to fast track God's will? Joseph is a wonderful example of a person who kept faith with God through difficult times and saw the prophetic word over his life fulfilled just when it seemed it was never going to happen! (See Genesis 37-50.)

So satan knows Scripture, probably better than you and I. The question is: *Where is the Word of God?* Is it in my heart or just in my understanding? Academic (or *theological*) debate is futile. What is God saying to His people? That is what we should be doing. Satan can use theology to bring division and draw God's people away from the Truth. That is why the Bible talks of *strange doctrines* (1 Tim. 1:3), *doctrines of demons* (1 Tim. 4:1), *children...carried about by every wind of doctrine, by the trickery of men, by craftiness in deceitful scheming* (Eph. 4:14). Satan uses Scripture to lead people from the Truth by distorting it. Such teachings bring death to the church. The life of God is lost. People find themselves in bondage. They begin to lose their faith. Every leader needs to watch over his life. Paul told the elders of the church in Ephesus to be on the alert:

> *Be on guard for yourselves and for all the flock, among which the Holy Spirit has made you overseers, to shepherd the church of God, which He purchased with His own blood. I know that after my departure savage wolves will come in among you, not sparing the flock; and from among your own selves men will arise, speaking perverse things, to draw away the disciples after them. There-fore be on the alert, remembering that night and day for a period of three years I did not cease to admonish each one with tears. And now I commend you to*

God and to the word of His grace, which is able to build you up and to give you the inheritance among all those who are sanctified (Acts 20:28-32).

You see, those who break away are often assumed to be in the wrong. Paul warns the elders at Ephesus that wolves will arise from among them. That kind of thing has to be watched. Diotrophes is an example of a man who operated in wrong leadership (see 3 John 1:9-11). The church has too frequently lost its way because it allowed wrong attitudes to rise up unchallenged. Leadership accountability both within the church and to an outside ministry helps safeguard against these things…it's also biblical.

This does not mean that breakaway groups are always right! Cults have arisen on occasions when the church of God was in a poor state but what was new did not represent God. It was a philosophy based on what they didn't like in the previous environment. Other groups have separated from the establishment purely on the basis that they found things in the church to be ungodly and unchanging.

So keep these things in mind:

- Guard your relationship with God.

- Practice His presence.

- Stay filled with the Spirit.

- Be accountable to others, even if you are a church pastor or the founder of a ministry.

- Make sure others "under you" know where your accountability lies.

Satan seeks to isolate. He succeeded with Eve. He tried with Jesus. He tries with us too. As I write this passage a man has called at the front door of my home. The backcloth to what he says is that he has the truth. We all need to be careful. The assumption that I have the truth and do not need the input of others is arrogance. We stand-alone; we become vulnerable to the enemy. He knows the Scriptures better than we do: but he does not know the Author! We don't know God because we belong to a great church or a wonderful movement. We only know Him through the Spirit in us. The antagonistic quoting of verses, the unwillingness to listen to others who also know the Spirit of Truth takes us into a dangerous place where satan can attack us in our isolation.

CONCLUSION

The Gospel of Matthew proves that satan can quote Scripture. Matthew's interpretation shows that God's people can be inspired by His Spirit and gain fresh revelation about things we thought we already knew. It is only the Spirit who will guide us into further Truth and protect us from the doctrines of demons and general satanic influence on theology. We need the Holy Spirit.

Chapter Twelve

PAUL'S EPISTLES

Words such as hypocrisy remind us that life and Truth go hand in hand. Paul was never a hypocrite and the unfolding of his life reveals to us the Truth process that went on in him. Even if our calls and gifts differ from his, that same progression applies to us. It's the same process of Truth that operates in all believers by the same Spirit. Knowing this, passages in the New Testament take on a different meaning:

> As you therefore have received Christ Jesus the Lord, so walk in Him, having been firmly rooted and now being built up in Him and established in your faith, just as you were instructed, and overflowing with gratitude. See to it that no one takes you captive through philosophy and empty deception, according to the tradition of men, according to the elementary principles of the world, rather than according to Christ (Colossians 2:6-8).

We received Christ by the Spirit. We continue to grow in Him in the same way. According to Paul in this passage, other things take us into captivity; it is the Spirit who sets us free.

At the beginning of to Book of Acts, Paul is well established in his understanding and theology of godly practices. He describes himself as being zealous: *"I am a Jew, born in Tarsus of Cilicia, but brought up in this city, educated under Gamaliel, strictly according to the law of our fathers, being zealous for God, just as you all are today"* (Acts 22:3). His teaching was in place and his life was mapped out.

Then he met Jesus on the Damascus road. It was the experience, not the theology that changed him. What we know about him is this: once he encountered Jesus and was taken to Damascus, his attitude to life and his own future was totally overturned as a direct result of his experience. After that we know he spent time in Arabia. Paul can sum everything we are examining here up in his letter to the Galatians:

> *But when He who had set me apart, even from my mother's womb, and called me through His grace, was pleased to reveal His Son in me, that I might preach Him among the Gentiles, I did not immediately consult with flesh and blood, nor did I go up to Jerusalem to those who were apostles before me; but I went away to Arabia, and returned once more to Damascus. Then three years later I went up to Jerusalem to become acquainted with Cephas, and stayed with him fifteen days* (Galatians 1:15-18).

The full context of this passage also mentions that Paul received his teaching during that time in Arabia—with no human agent present. So his theology came by revelation of the Spirit. Later, he confirmed it with the other apostles in Jerusalem (see Gal. 2:2).

This means that everything Paul did and wrote began with his experience of God through the Spirit. To put it in simple terms, he continued in the way and revelation of the Spirit that he received on the Damascus road. It seems as if Paul didn't spend time studying the Old Testament to get something *from the Word*. His epistles were written from his heart expressing contemporary Truth into immediate situations; he wrote what the Spirit gave him.

In this chapter, Paul's writings will be examined to note any comparison or contrast with the Old Testament Scriptures that he knew so well.

GALATIANS

I really like what Rick Joyner writes in his book *The Apostolic Ministry* when he says that, "Since the Reformation, we have used Paul to interpret Jesus rather than the other way round. The true foundations of Christian truth are the teachings of Jesus, not Paul."[1] This principle is so important to our understanding of how we should receive and interpret Scripture. For too long we have majored in the Epistles instead of the teachings of the One who is the Head of the Church!

When we look at the teaching brought by Jesus, we realize it was sometimes to individuals or groupings:

❖ The twelve.

❖ The scribes and Pharisees.

❖ The crowds.

❖ People like the rich young ruler, Nicodemus, etc.

However, much of what He said carried the wider aspect of universal declaration. The teachings of Jesus were unlike the writers of the Epistles that rather addressed specific situations and therefore carried some teaching that would not necessarily apply to every other situation, even if they were similar.

The example of Paul's Epistle to the Galatians helps us understand this difference. Paul's letter was written to a situation where teachers have caused difficulties by insisting that all the men in the church should be circumcised. We know from elsewhere in the New Testament (Acts 15) that this was not insisted upon at all by the Council of Apostles and Elders who met in Jerusalem. Today, that kind of corrective teaching brought by Paul would not necessarily apply to many of our church, denominational, or regional situations. However, as with all the other Epistles, there are still principles that can and need to be applied to our situations today. At the same time we can consider whether our attitude toward deviant teaching, contrary to the Gospel, is right.

Circumcision

I knew a church minister years ago who decided his baby son should be circumcised. I also recall a teenager in one city where we lived who had to be hospitalized because, having read the Bible, he decided he should also be circumcised, so he did it himself—the results were disastrous.

The above examples probably speak of something that is very rare since the New Testament teachings make it clear that circumcision is not a requirement for Gentile believers. I mention them so that we understand that any of us can misinterpret Scripture, especially when we live a fairly isolated, unaccountable life and act almost entirely on our own initiative (totally unlike Jesus). We can get ideas in our heads and just run with them.

The New Testament does not insist on circumcision. Jewish believers went into the church at Antioch and taught that circumcision was a needful act. As a result, men were sent to Jerusalem to discuss with the Apostles there about the subject. The result of those discussions was that the Gentiles should only subject themselves on the following basis:

> For it seemed good to the Holy Spirit and to us to lay upon you no greater burden than these essentials: that you abstain from things sacrificed to idols and from blood and from things strangled and from fornication; if you keep yourselves free from such things, you will do well (Acts 15:28-29).

So there was no mention of circumcision as a necessary act for the Gentile believers.

It is obvious that much discussion and debate took place before a decision was reached. However, perhaps we should also notice here the important phrase *"seemed good to the Holy Spirit and to us."* The decision was more than a good one. They trusted the Holy Spirit to take them into the Truth. So, at the end of the debate, the question was not answered on a political basis, nor was it compromise. It was a decision based on what the Spirit said.

Circumcision and Spirit

Now all this ties in with Galatians in more than one way. The problem in that church was doctrinal but it was also spiritual. Doctrinal error results from us straying from the Holy Spirit—the Spirit of Truth. Paul shows that the root of the situation in the Galatian church was a spiritual one rather than one of understanding. This is clear from very early on in the Epistle. Paul writes:

> *I am amazed that you are so quickly deserting Him who called you by the grace of Christ, for a different gospel; which is really not another; only there are some who are disturbing you, and want to distort the gospel of Christ* (Galatians 1:6,7).

What Paul says in these few words is critical:

❖ The Galatians are deserting Jesus.

❖ They are following false teaching.

❖ There are "teachers" who have distorted the Gospel.

❖ They have disturbed the church.

This really needs some comment. First of all I do wonder how much the 21st century church would state or even recognize the wrong doctrinal basis for what was happening. I think we would tend to tolerate the actions and teachings of others for the sake of peace and unity. Paul takes a very different perspective on what was happening. In the same chapter of Galatians (verse 10), Paul further comments: *"For am I now seeking the favor of men, or of God? Or am I striving to please men? If I were still trying to please men, I would not be a bond-servant of Christ."* He is clear that his ministry is not one of compromise.

False teaching has twisted and weakened the Truth of the Gospel. The evidence for that is how the people are, not just what they believe and practice. It has to do with the heart—again! The teachers coming from Jerusalem to the Galatians brought a Gospel that was distorted. The distortion comes from the heart—the seat of truth and error. The pure in heart do not distort the Truth. They cannot if their heart source is one of purity. This also means that the true ministry of a teacher is from the heart, not the head. So he speaks from revelation, not research.

Paul's theology changed dramatically from the moment he was saved. Everything he believed and practiced came under immediate scrutiny and transformation as a direct result of his experience of Jesus in that moment. Whatever it was, it changed where it needed to, and the change was internal to him, not just in his mind. That transformation permeated his life so what he later wrote in his Epistles was not the result of study; it all ensued from revelation by the Spirit.

The specific matter of what Paul wrote on circumcision becomes even more fascinating when we look at his practice. It shows us how theology has to be in submission to the Spirit.

When Timothy traveled with him, Paul had him circumcised. This is how the Bible puts it:

> *And he came also to Derbe and to Lystra. And behold, a certain disciple was there, named Timothy, the son of a Jewish woman who was a believer, but his father was a Greek, and he was well spoken of by the brethren who were in Lystra and Iconium. Paul wanted this man to go with him; and he took him and circumcised him because of the Jews who were in those parts, for they all knew that his father was a Greek (Acts 16:1-3).*

Why would Paul go against his theology? There is only one answer—*the Spirit told him to.* There is no other basis. However, this shows that the Holy Spirit can operate (and through people) outside Scripture. It also says that the Truth Paul lived by was in the Spirit, not the letter. We can argue intellectually and make suggestions as to why Timothy should be circumcised. If we do that, we immediately complicate things. We attempt to justify what Paul sensed in the Spirit. When we question Paul, we also question ourselves and our church situations. We neglect what the Spirit is saying and opt for answers and decisions based on human wisdom.

Any other way of looking at this matter also implies an inconsistency in Paul's life that does not accord with reality. Luke writes of the circumcision of Timothy without question, but if there is any other person who can be seen in similar light to Timothy, it is Titus. They were both given similar responsibilities by Paul to establish local church leadership. Titus, like Timothy, was uncircumcised. Yet when he went with Paul to Jerusalem, he was not required to submit himself to the rite (see Gal. 2:1-3). You see, we cannot take one instance and produce a doctrine. Things didn't happen like that in New Testament times. They did what was right according to the Spirit. We can learn to do the same.

THE LAW

We all understand that Paul was well versed in the Law. He taught it. Once he became a follower of Christ, his life changed. However, he was well qualified to comment on the Law in the light of the Gospel.

We can take as an example of Paul's attitude to the Law from 1 Timothy 1:5-12:

> But the goal of our instruction is love from a pure heart and a good conscience and a sincere faith. For some men, straying from these things, have turned aside to fruitless discussion, wanting to be teachers of the Law, even though they do not understand either what they are saying or the matters about which they make confident assertions. But we know that the Law is good, if one uses it lawfully, realizing the fact that law is not made for a righteous man, but for those who are lawless and rebellious, for the ungodly and sinners, for the unholy and profane, for those who kill their fathers or mothers, for murderers and immoral men and homosexuals and kidnappers and liars and perjurers, and whatever else is contrary to sound teaching, according to the glorious gospel of the blessed God, with which I have been entrusted. I thank Christ Jesus our Lord, who has strengthened me, because He considered me faithful, putting me into service.

Notice the phrase *"the law is not made for a righteous man."* This fact is clear throughout the Old Testament. It was because Abraham believed God that he was deemed to be righteous. He lied about his wife more than once, but did not lose his righteousness because it was God-given. By faith Noah obtained righteousness, but he did not lose it when he became drunk. Moses brought the Law to the people: but he wasn't perfect. He was a murderer. Yet he had intimacy with God. Oh that we all might learn this Truth!

We are made righteous in Christ (see Rom. 3:22; 10:4; Phil. 3:9); and it is based on our faith. Since the law was not made for a righteous man, that means it was not made for us if we are in Christ.

This is not to say that we can do whatever we want whenever we want to. Paul makes that clear in Romans chapter 6. What is does mean is that imperfection does not disqualify us from our righteousness, because it is based in Christ and not in ourselves. So the Truth we live is in the Spirit, in Christ. We are representatives of God and of Christ and the earth not of the Law.

Paul makes it clear we have come to a better place. In Galatians he differentiates between two mountains—Sinai and Zion. Sinai is the place where the Law was given to Moses. Zion is the place of rejoicing and victory. This is what he says:

> *For it is written that Abraham had two sons, one by the bondwoman and one by the free woman. But the son by the bondwoman was born according to the flesh, and the son by the free woman through the promise. This is allegorically speaking: for these women are two covenants, one proceeding from Mount Sinai bearing children who are to be slaves; she is Hagar. Now this Hagar is Mount Sinai in Arabia, and corresponds to the present Jerusalem, for she is in slavery with her children. But the Jerusalem above is free; she is our mother* (Galatians 4:22-26).

This is about Abraham's two sons and the women with whom he had them. The first, Ishmael, was the son of Hagar. He was born into slavery because his mother was a bondwoman. Isaac was the faith son, the son of the promise. Paul relates these two relationships with Abraham to the two mountains—Sinai and Zion. The first covenant is the Mosaic one it speaks of law. The second speaks of Sonship, because Isaac was the son of the promise of God. That is why Paul says: *"the Jerusalem from above is free; she is our **mother**."* When we become born again we enter into that Sonship, leaving behind us the domain of the Law. We come out of our sinfulness into freedom. That is our status in Christ—children of God.

The whole matter is best summed up in Romans 8 where Paul writes, *"There is therefore now no condemnation for those who are in Christ Jesus. For the law of the Spirit of life in Christ Jesus has set you free from the law of sin and of death"* (Rom. 8:1-2). The new law in Christ is by the Spirit of God. It brings life and sets us free from the condemnation to death as a result of sin. Its foundation is the grace of God that is discovered by faith and apportions righteousness to us. Therefore the new law for us is practiced by experiencing the Spirit in our lives. So it is the *law of the Spirit of life* under which we now live.

Conclusion

Paul's letters are based on his own experience that began on the way to Damascus. He was taught by the Spirit to live in the same Spirit. His view of the Scriptures he knew so well was transformed because of the Spirit of Truth. Experience of the Spirit changed his life and theology. From that encounter on the road to Damascus, Paul's theology and his experience of God were one and the same.

Endnote

1. Rick Joyner, *The Apostolic Ministry* (Fort Mill, SC: MorningStar, 1004), 47.

Chapter Thirteen

JOHN'S WRITINGS

From my early days as a Christian, I felt that John's Gospel was the best! I liked it because it didn't *just tell a story!* I liked it because it was *deeper* and I preferred things more scholarly because I considered myself an academic. In fact, before becoming born again, I argued in a high school religious study class against the physical resurrection of Jesus because at the time I felt it was fun.

My early understanding of John's Gospel was so shallow that I failed to recognize the basis on which he wrote his contribution to the New Testament. It did not help that in those early days I was part of a church that enjoyed the intellectual appeal of Bible study. I was wrong in so many ways about so many things. I do not believe our minds have to be our worst enemy. I just know that they can be either our worst enemy or our best friend in the same day!

THE GOSPEL

From the beginning of John's Gospel it is clear that he is writing an intimate account of the continuous living union between Jesus and the Father:

"...the Word became flesh, and dwelt among us, and we beheld His glory, glory as of the only begotten from the Father, full of grace and truth (John 1:14).

Many of us would traditionally speak mainly from this verse on the concept that the Word became flesh. It's certainly important, but John says more. He states that Jesus lived (dwelt) among us! We saw (beheld) His glory. It was real and experiential. So the Word becoming flesh was part of the disciples' life experience of three years with Jesus. The impact was not so much the teaching; it was the Son of God Himself. His teaching was not separate from Him. He spoke from who He was. His being and teaching were one and the same.

This is not to say we should ignore all that has been rightly said and written about this Gospel. My point is that we tend to overlook the valuable experiences that touched hearts and lives and inspired writings that form the New Testament.

Initiative

I attended a leaders' conference in the United Kingdom in the early 1980s where I heard the keynote speaker talk about Jesus' submission to the Father. At that time, it was no more than a concept for me. These days I have come to realize that I like Jesus, need to live under the guidance of God by the leading of the Spirit in me.

There are six occasions in John's Gospel (in the New American Standard Bible) where Jesus states that He does nothing on His own initiative (see John 5:30; 8:28,42; 10:18, 12:49 and 14:10). This is with regard to His ministry, what He says and what He does. His relationship with the Father and the Spirit led Him. What this means for us is that as children of God we are also led by the Spirit (see Rom. 8:14). Since the Holy Spirit is the Spirit of Truth, we understand that the only way we live the Truth as Jesus did is by being led of the Spirit. The initiative is His, not ours. John's writings specifically help us to understand this.

Over the years, I have been cautious to move in grace. Many times people wronged me. I did not react. I stayed silent. Quite unexpectedly in recent months, the Holy Spirit has been speaking to me differently. He has told me to make a defense of myself in specific situations. This does not mean that I was wrong in the past to stay silent. It also does not mean that the Holy Spirit contradicts Himself. It is a matter of hearing the voice of the Spirit so that when things change in the divine will, we are ready to implement that change. Jesus said that His time had not yet come. By the Spirit we can know the now of God. This is essential to us if we are to move in the miraculous and bring the supernatural wisdom of God into all kinds of situations.

PASTORAL

Peter and John together spent special time with Jesus. Although they were particularly close to Him, they were so different. Peter comes across in the Gospels and Acts as a man of action. John is a more quiet man, working behind the scenes. When Jesus first meets them, they are fishermen. Peter is in the act of fishing; John is mending the nets with his father—indicating that Peter likes to do while John is concerned with unity, love, and fellowship. John is motivated by the pastoral life among the believers and this aspect is evident in his New Testament writings.

For example, he writes of Jesus as the Good Shepherd (see John 10:11,14). In the same passage Jesus expands on what is meant by "shepherd":

> ...even as the Father knows Me and I know the Father; and I lay down My life for the sheep. And I have other sheep, which are not of this fold; I must bring them also, and they shall hear My voice; and they shall become one flock with one shepherd. "For this reason the Father loves Me, because I lay down My life that I may take it again. "No one has taken it away from Me, but I lay it down on My own initiative. I have authority to lay it down, and I have authority to take it up again. This commandment I received from My Father (John 10:15-18).

This speaks of a selfless life given to God and then to people. Jesus used the authority given to Him by the Father to lay down His personal well-being. This is the shepherd, laying down his life for the sheep.

Yet when we see our role model Shepherd in action, He doesn't seem to be what we see today in His followers. If everything Jesus did was subject to His Father's will, if He only did what He saw the Father do, if He only said what He heard the Father say, then the pastoral care exercised by Jesus was by the Spirit. In that case, ours should be too.

In many ways, we have reduced pastoral care to common sense. In everyday case scenarios we may have even used it as a means of control, causing people to be manipulated to fit in with what we want. Trust in pastoral care must be by the Spirit; otherwise it is not operating from Truth. When we move by the Spirit to handle difficulties, then pastoral care takes much less time!

Here are a few examples from my own experience:

"I'm not going to waste God's time or mine by praying for you!" I said this many years ago when I was part of a mid-week Bible study in a church that was without a pastor. At the end of the meeting a woman approached me. She asked advice, and I advised her. A few weeks later I was in another meeting at the same church. I was there on a Sunday morning to preach with a hope of becoming pastor of that church.

At the end of the meeting, the woman who had talked with me after the Bible study came to me again. She talked about the same things we discussed a few weeks earlier.

"What do you expect me to do for you," I asked her.

"I want you to pray for me."

"I'll do no such thing," I said.

"I thought you were supposed to be a Pastor," she said angrily.

"You can think whatever you like. You talked this over with me a few weeks ago and it's clear you haven't followed through on the advice I gave you. I'm not going to waste God's time or mine by praying for you."

Notice the reply of the woman, *"I thought you were supposed to be...."* People frequently have wrong expectations about what pastoral care really is.

That is not the end of the story. I didn't realize that while I was talking with her, another woman was watching me from a distance. She saw how I handled her; she immediately went to a member of the church Board and told him, *"That's the man we need here."* I later found out that the woman talking with me had been a major cause of problems in the church.

Sometimes the problem we are trying to handle is the person we are speaking with, not just the situation itself!

I'll tell you exactly what God told me...

There was a woman who was a member of a church I once led. She suffered terribly from epileptic fits that would suddenly come upon her. Her medical condition was so bad that she was on heavy medication. Her body was so full of drugs she was not allowed to have children.

One particularly Sunday during the service, she had a fit just as we were about to break bread. Two strong young men carried her from the meeting into a side room. My full-time assistant stayed there with her for the rest of the service. We called her unsaved husband and her doctor to come to her.

When the service was over, I went to the side room were my assistant was praying and rebuking the devil. He asked for my help, but I just left the room. Something was bothering me. I had no peace in my spirit.

A few minutes later the husband and doctor arrived and tended to the woman. She was given an injection and both men helped her to her husband's car. The doctor returned to the church building to collect his bag. As he was leaving, I asked him *to what extent can these things be self-inflicted?* He told me that it was possible for that to be the case. He also added that if I could help him with that particular case, he would be very grateful.

That afternoon I received a call on behalf of the woman asking to see me that same day. I waited until God told me to go to her. The rest of Sunday passed by and Monday too; Tuesday afternoon I went to visit her.

I asked the woman a few times if she brought on the fits herself. She insisted no and became angry. She then became extremely irate. And started shouting.

I responded loudly: "I'll tell you exactly what God told me. When you were 12 years old your mother had another baby girl and from that moment on you started manifesting fits. Don't try to tell me I'm lying!"

The woman broke down. Sobbing, she admitted the truth. She repented, came off medication at a rapid rate, was allowed to have children (she had two) and her husband became saved. Of course he did. He had seen God move! This was a pastoral situation solved by the Spirit.

I am not saying that all epileptic fits result from the same source. I am saying that every pastoral matter should be handled according to the leading of the Spirit. No two situations are identical.

Ananias and Sapphira

Most are familiar with Ananias and Sapphira in the early church. This was a pastoral situation that appeared to be fine but the wrong was brought to light and handled by the Spirit. (See Acts 5:1-11.)

Pastoral care—just like prophecy, it's by the fruit we recognize the gift of God. It takes great courage to handle things in this way when dealing with pastoral matters. It's not always gentleness that wins (nor is it bullying tactics!). But moving in the Spirit may cause us to deal with church situations in ways that are only justified by the end result.

The Epistles

Most of the content of John's letters has to do with loving one another and practicing unity and fellowship. The foundation on which he writes these things is summed up at the beginning of his first Epistle:

> *What was from the beginning, what we have heard, what we have seen with our eyes, what we beheld and our hands handled, concerning the Word of Life—and the life was manifested, and we have seen and bear witness and proclaim to you the eternal life, which was with the Father and was manifested to us—what we have seen and heard we proclaim to you also, that you also may have fellowship with us; and indeed our fellowship is with the Father, and with His Son Jesus Christ* (1 John 1:1-3)

John speaks of the senses. He says:

❖ We have *heard.*

❖ We have *seen* with our eyes.

❖ Our *hands* have handled.

❖ The *life* was manifested.

❖ We have *seen* and *bear witness.*

John is writing out of experience with Jesus, not doctrine. It's the experience of the disciples as they spent three years with the Savior. He writes of what they saw and experienced. It is real, not just concepts.

Over recent years I have stressed to people the need to follow through on talking with the one in the church who has wronged them. People give many reasons why they think it is not possible to face the person or the church. As leaders, if we live it, then we can teach it. If we live it, but don't teach it, then we are being hypocritical and in compromise. Not only must I live what I teach, I must also teach what I live! Whatever your current position, according to the teachings of Jesus in Matthew 18, we will never achieve the unity He prayed for if we do not come in line with His basic teaching on the practicalities of Church unity.

John's writings bring the Spirit of Truth through revealing the Word of life, love in action, encouragement and counsel—so our *"joy may be full."* (See 1,2,3 John.)

CONCLUSION

John wrote about what he lived and experienced. He, like other New Testament writers, wrote to the Church from his strengths in God. Those writers were not competitive. John wrote from his relationship with Jesus. So, too, did Paul. John wrote to specific churches and individuals where he was involved as an apostle. God's Truth only becomes truth to us when we experience it through revelation of the Spirit.

Part Five

THE TRUTH OF KNOWLEDGE

AND THEY SHALL NOT TEACH EVERYONE HIS FELLOW CITIZEN, AND
EVERYONE HIS BROTHER SAYING, "KNOW THE LORD" FOR ALL WILL
KNOW ME, FROM THE LEAST TO THE GREATEST OF THEM

(Hebrews 8:11).

Chapter Fourteen

CONFESSION

Truth seems to be illusive when it works for some and not for others. Over years, many people have taught, practiced, and have become confused and discouraged by "confession." Confusion leads to division because experience lines up with Truth—our theology tends to line up with our experience. So why does confession seem to yield results for some and not others?

An essential passage helps us understand:

> But what does it say? "THE WORD IS NEAR YOU, IN YOUR MOUTH AND IN YOUR HEART"—that is, the word of faith which we are preaching, that if you confess with your mouth Jesus as Lord, and believe in your heart that God raised Him from the dead, you shall be saved; for with the heart man believes, resulting in righteousness, and with the mouth he confesses, resulting in salvation. For the Scripture says, "WHOEVER BELIEVES IN HIM WILL NOT BE DISAPPOINTED" (Romans 10:8-11).

Where the Word Is

Paul clearly says that the Word is not only in our mouths but also in our hearts. Throughout this book I've shared that the real seat of Truth is our hearts. Whatever we may confess with our mouths is empty words unless it originates in our hearts.

Many people I have met over the years have told me that they did what they were told through the teaching they received to "confess" the Truth (perhaps by quoting Scripture). This practice will only be effective if confession starts in the heart. Truth is more than the citing of words. Biblical confession includes conviction of the Truth expressed from a genuine heart.

This is not to criticize those who have taught effectively about confession. Such teachers I have heard genuinely expressed Truth based on their own experience. They have lived it from the heart. If we are also to live it, then effective confession will only come as an expression of our relationship with God and our own conviction deep within our own hearts.

What Is Taught

This is what Paul preaches. His public expression of Truth is based on the Word in his heart and his experience of it in his daily life. For centuries, most teaching has had as its base concepts ideas and theologies that were passed from one intellect to another. This is a broad generalization, but what it produced was students instead of disciples. Many books written over the years convey information without perhaps provoking the readers to experience in the Spirit the Truth contained in the writings.

What was taught by Paul and other writers of the New Testament was based on experiences of the Spirit that had brought Truth to them. So the teaching comes from the heart of the teacher and has as its destination the heart of the reader or listener.

The Basis

The kind of teaching quoted by Paul produces *righteousness*. God's Truth and righteousness co-exist. If you have one, you have both. Paul tells us that when we put on the *"new self"* then we become like God, *"created in righteousness and holiness of the truth"* (Eph. 4:24).

The Bible tells God's people that. *"He made Him* [Jesus] *who knew no sin to be sin on our behalf, that we might become the righteousness of God in Him"* (2 Cor. 5:21). Our basis of righteousness is not personal perfection; it is only through the work of Jesus in His death on the Cross. When we became born again, our belief in Jesus caused God to attribute to us righteousness because we became *in Christ.* That means we are righteous since we are *in* His righteousness.

Paul expresses this clearly earlier in Romans when he writes:

> *For I am not ashamed of the gospel, for it is the power of God for salvation to everyone who believes, to the Jew first and also to the Greek. For in it the righteousness of God is revealed from faith to faith as it is written, "BUT THE RIGHTEOUS man SHALL LIVE BY FAITH."* (Romans 1:16-17).

The phrase *"from faith to faith"* brings us into the next aspect to consider.

BELIEF

The passages in Romans 1 and 10 bring in the element of faith and tell us that salvation comes to us because *"with the heart man believes."* There is no point in confessing what we do not believe. Some say to maintain confession in order to bring the heart to the point of conviction. I would say that kind of confession is based on *"Lord, I believe, help my unbelief."* There is a good desire to reach the place of activated faith.

The same mouth that confesses can also deny. Peter confessed, *"Thou art the Christ, the Son of the living God."* (Matt. 16:16). That was a genuine confession of his heart toward Jesus. Moments later his speech was demonically inspired. The infamous relevance in Peter's life is his triple denial of Jesus. Jesus told him he would deny Him three times. Jesus also said that if we deny Him before men He would also deny us before His Father. In Peter's case, grace in the heart of Jesus (from the Father) was greater than the words Jesus had spoken (also from the Father). The Spirit goes beyond the letter of the Word.

I remember as a young believer living in genuine fear of denying Jesus. Peter did it, but he also found restoration because God knew his heart. It's worth remembering that one mistake does not undo our salvation. Belief in the heart still stands even when the mouth may not be confessing it! However, that does not necessarily work the other way round. As with Peter, the Holy Spirit often restores us when He whispers on behalf of Jesus...*Do you love Me?* (See Chapter 2.)

"... *not everyone who says to me...*" has been discussed in Chapter 5 so there is nothing to add except to show how the Scripture ties in with the practice.

Two things have to line up:

❖ Integrity of heart.

❖ Genuine faith from the heart toward God.

CONCLUSION

God looks at your heart, not the deed. Our theology of God is based on our experience of Him. The seat of Truth, genuine theology, is, therefore, the heart.

Chapter Fifteen

SEPARATION

Whenever we pursue the Truth, there is always the possibility of separation. The Bible tells us that the Truth is like a sword—a sword that divides:

> *For the word of God is living and active and sharper than any two-edged sword, and piercing as far as the division of soul and spirit, of both joints and marrow, and able to judge the thoughts and intentions of the heart* (Hebrews 4:12).

Scripture also states that the Word of God is *"the sword of the Spirit"* (Eph. 6:17).

The Hebrews passage says that God's Word pierces *"as far as the division of soul and spirit"*; it separates! However, we also established in a previous chapter that God's Word alone does not bring change by application of the Truth. That is essentially the work of the Spirit. So the activity that brings the Word of God to bear is through the Holy Spirit. Ephesians informs us that God's word is the *sword* of the Spirit.

Over the years I've known quite a few people who got involved in the sport of fencing. I don't know much about it, but I do know this: *the fencer (or person holding the sword) is in charge of the weapon.* This means some of our thinking has to change regarding the *sword* of the Spirit. When I set out to write this book, a lady I've known for quite a few years advised me to be careful because whatever the Spirit did was subject to the Scriptures. This is classic teaching, particularly concerning the moving of the Spirit. The real concern that causes such statements to be made has nothing to do with a lack of trust of the Holy Spirit; it is more likely an awareness of believers moving in the flesh instead of the Spirit. This unfortunately does happen, but in the New Testament it is dealt with *without quenching the Spirit* (see 1 Thess. 5:19) and the same should happen in the Church today.

We have already seen in a previous chapter, that Jesus didn't stick firmly to the literal Law as interpreted by the Jews of His day. We must also recognize that the Holy Spirit is the *author* of the Scriptures. He inspired those who wrote down the Word of God. He is not subject to the Scriptures. He guides us into all the Truth; He cannot be subject to what He wrote, the sword that He wields. The Holy Spirit is in charge.

It is in this light we need to consider the verses that say: *Not that we are adequate in ourselves to consider anything as coming from ourselves, but our adequacy is from God, who also made us adequate as servants of a new covenant, not of the letter, but of the Spirit; for the letter kills, but the Spirit gives life* (2 Cor. 3:5-6).

Paul speaks of his ministry in this passage he wrote to the church in Corinth. This former Pharisee, teacher of the Law taught by Gamaliel, no longer operates according to the letter of the Scriptures. He has come to operate in a ministry that is Spirit-based and superior to what he knew before. Paul had passed from Law to grace, from letter to Spirit. We should do the same—we have passed from death to life, from darkness to light. If we are to stand for the Truth, then we should be taking what we know of the Word in order to operate in the Holy Sprit. In this way we leave behind the killing letter of literalism and move to the Word becoming flesh in us. Truth is based in our now experience of God through the Spirit.

Paul and Barnabas

People are often criticized for separating themselves. But sometimes there are good reasons why they do so. When Paul and Barnabas separated from one another, the Bible tells us:

And there arose such a sharp disagreement that they separated from one an-
other, and Barnabas took Mark with him and sailed away to Cyprus. But
Paul chose Silas and departed, being committed by the brethren to the grace
of the Lord (Acts 15:39-40).

The word translated here as *"a sharp disagreement"* really means, "sharp-ening." This definition helps us. It seems that both Paul and Barnabas had the Truth for what they should do. As they debated, each one sharpened the other's conviction. They did separate. The separation was not perma-nent. Paul was right about what John Mark had done. Barnabas was right to take him along because John Mark was, indeed, restored.

Let's establish these findings:

❖ Each man operated from his own conviction (see Rom. 14:5; 1 Cor. 7:7).

❖ The difference in direction of the two was based in friendship when iron sharpens iron. They went separate ways. Like two pieces of iron rubbing against each other, both are sharpened as a result (see Prov. 27:17).

❖ Paul and Barnabas worked together again (see 1 Cor. 9:6).

❖ Mark was restored and worked with both Barnabas and Paul (see Col. 4:10).

I wonder how many of us have taken a position of criticism toward someone's change in direction without any consideration as to why they should be moving on. The least we should do is talk about it with them. This is particularly sad when people are genuinely pursuing the Truth. In-stead of expressing dissatisfaction we should be contenders for the faith and for the Truth. When we do this we may also be in for criticism, but we stand for the Truth.

PAUL AT EPHESUS (See Acts 19.)

There is another example of purposeful separation in the life of Paul. In many ways, this is more controversial in the current climate of church life and thinking.

When Paul arrived in Ephesus, he found *"some disciples."* As he talked with them he realized that although they were indeed disciples, they had not received two experiences considered essential in New Testament teaching. Therefore he took them further into the Truth by administering baptism in water and the baptism of the Spirit. They received the Spirit in a similar way as Peter and others had received Him on the Day of Pentecost (see Acts 19:2-6). This was evidence that Paul had done the right thing.

Paul was not in Ephesus to bring separation. He was an ambassador for the Truth. He spent three months in the synagogue teaching, reasoning, and persuading with boldness. His purpose was to unite all in the synagogue in the experience and understanding of the Truth by sharing with them what he had received.

Toward the end of the three months, some began to oppose him and his teaching, and were *"becoming hardened and disobedient, speaking evil of the Way before the multitude"* (Acts 19:9). It was because of this that Paul withdrew and took the disciples with him. Since some opposed the Truth and spoke evil, Paul had to contend for that Truth. It may be that the opposition came for some other reason, but it's more likely the opposition was to Paul's teaching on water baptism, or the baptism in the Holy Spirit—or both. At that stage, the separation safeguarded the Truth. It was right at that moment.

This kind of separation does happen from time to time. In the 1920s in the United Kingdom, people were forced to depart from some denominational churches because they had received the baptism in the Spirit. In the 1970s fresh revelation came to some about the ministry gifts of Christ mentioned in Ephesians 4:11. In both of these cases, the separation came to embrace the new revelation. Experience of God had established the teaching from the Word in the lives of some believers. They also set up separate organizations (some were probably necessary, others perhaps not). Today both truths for which believers had to contend (particularly baptism in the Spirit) are widely accepted among the church groups that once opposed them. It would also be true to say that many of those churches of a more traditional background have advanced beyond those who originally broke fresh ground. Truth is alive.

We need to be experiencing the living Truth so that we do not fall behind others who catch the revelation we have already embraced! The sad thing is that those who originally broke ranks for the revelation they received sometimes find it difficult to accept that other churches or church groups can move in the same thing. God owns revelation, not the person or people who originally receive it.

Jesus and Division

Jesus also spoke graphically about His own ministry and the division it would cause:

> *Do not think that I came to bring peace on the earth; I did not come to bring peace, but a sword. For I came to SET A MAN AGAINST HIS FATHER, AND A DAUGHTER AGAINST HER MOTHER, AND A DAUGHTER-IN-LAW AGAINST HER MOTHER-IN-LAW; and A MAN'S ENEMIES WILL BE THE MEMBERS OF HIS HOUSEHOLD. He who loves father or mother more than Me is not worthy of Me; and he who loves son or daughter more than Me is not worthy of Me. And he who does not take his cross and follow after Me is not worthy of Me. He who has found his life shall lose it, and he who has lost his life for My sake shall find it. He who receives you receives Me, and he who receives Me receives Him who sent Me. He who receives a prophet in the name of a prophet shall receive a prophet's reward; and he who receives a righteous man in the name of a righteous man shall receive a righteous man's reward* (Matthew 10:34-41).

Briefly, the sword of the Spirit of Truth that Jesus brought would bring separation including:

❖ The removal of superficial peace.

❖ The breakdown of family relationships.

❖ The division of those who would receive a ministry of God (in the direct context, a prophet) and those who wouldn't.

The radical truth of all this—we know that Jesus only said what the Father told Him to say. Therefore when He spoke in John 6 about being the bread of life, He was speaking from the Father. As a result of what He said (the Truth), many disciples left Him. God's will was to challenge those who were shallowly following Jesus.

Examining John 6 in more detail, we find that Jesus made claims that ran contrary to what people understood. He said that He was the true manna coming down from Heaven. This statement advanced the Truth He had already declared—Jesus only said what He heard the Father say. There were times when Jesus, on the prompting of His Father, challenged those around Him to make decisions. The challenge was to separate more of the Truth as Jesus declared it. Those listening had only two options. Truth demands a response from us. How we respond depends on our sensitivity to the Holy Spirit; He alone will guide us into the Truth.

Power and effectiveness have nothing to do with numbers or size. Gideon had an army that was too big for God to be glorified. When the numbers were reduced on the command of God, the battle was won and it was clear that God gave the victory. Similarly, in John 6 Jesus lost many disciples but gained a different level of commitment. This made both Him and them more effective in doing the Father's will.

This is different from the division of forces in Acts 15 when Paul left with Silas, and Barnabas with Mark. There is, though, one principle to apply to both. God's will was in effect.

So what about us? As I write, I am conscious of some people I recently spoke with who felt led to lay down the leadership of the church they were leading. They had already talked with me once and still felt they should resign. They did so on the basis of the will of God. After that they came and showed me a letter written to them by the leader of the group of churches. It was a long letter. As I got to the end of the second paragraph, I handed the letter back because I didn't want to read any more. It was full of criticism and condemnation, and it carried an ungodly strength in it. It did not provoke faith.

The man writing the letter was well intentioned. He wanted them to continue to lead the church. What he wrote was not by the Spirit but from his own thoughts. If the leader had responded as the letter required, he would have continued in leadership and things would have become worse because he would be operating outside of his own faith and what the Holy Spirit was saying to him.

Putting it another way, the man would have departed from his spiritual integrity. Whether the decision of that leader was right or wrong is not the issue. In the New Testament, unless there is a word of knowledge or discerning of Spirit, there is no place for challenging the decisions of believers. We must learn—it's time to stop trying to do the work of the Holy Spirit for Him! We should *trust* the Spirit of God. Peter learned because he got it wrong, not because Jesus prevented him from making a mistake. Leadership in churches so often produces faith babies instead of allowing growth and maturity by learning through our mistakes. So as we learn to trust and obey the leading of the Spirit:

- ❖ He will lead us.

- ❖ We trust Him to lead others as well.

- ❖ The Spirit will guide all of us into all the Truth.

- ❖ God will cause all things (including the wrong decisions taken) to work together for our good.

- ❖ We understand that the final authority over all life is God's and He will do the right things.

- ❖ We do not have to move in the flesh against what we see to be wrong; everything should be handled under the guidance of the Spirit. Otherwise we respond to a wrong with another wrong!

- ❖ If God *does* want us to do something against what is wrong then He will show us by the Spirit.

Have you ever considered how Nathan handled David's sin against Uriah and Bathsheba? (See 2 Samuel 11-12.) David did all he could to hide his adulterous act including having the army withdraw from Uriah (Bathsheba's husband) while he was in the battle so that he would be killed. Nathan the prophet knew about David's deception but did not move to challenge him until prompted by God. We should do the same. If we are the children of God then His Spirit is leading us. We do not react because we don't like something; we wait for the prompting of God through the Spirit. As He leads, we operate in the Truth because He is the Spirit of Truth.

As we look at Jesus, the Truth, and separation, we see a relevancy between Jesus' decisions and our daily life. In the Kingdom we should not operate a blame culture. Managers in industry routinely seek to apportion blame for a mistake on a scapegoat. The Church should work differently.

Years ago I was held partly responsible for a situation that occurred in a church I was leading. The overseeing minister made sure the people in the church knew I hadn't been in perfect in the situation. It was true; I had made one mistake. A member challenged the overseer of the church, saying that I had been made a scapegoat. I remember so clearly that as soon as he said that, I immediately lined myself up with Jesus. In the Kingdom He has become the scapegoat. We should not be looking for someone to blame. Our task is to clear things up for God, not individuals.

When Jesus prays in John 17 He says to God that of those that He gave to Him, *"none was lost except the son of perdition"* (John 17:12). Judas Iscariot was the son of perdition and was chosen by Jesus to be with Him. It was His Father's choice. Naturally speaking it would seem a wrong choice, but there is no blame culture for Jesus! I was once asked if I felt I had made the wrong decision in appointing a certain man to an eldership position. I replied quoting the example of Judas. Did God make the wrong choice when He appointed Saul to be the first King of Israel? I don't think so.

With both Saul and Judas, separation was necessary. The experience helped godly people see how God works. In the Book of Numbers, God's people had to separate themselves from the sons of Korah in order to remain with God (see Num. 16:20). In this sense, separation is to God. We are separating ourselves from ungodliness (and lack of repentance) in order not to suffer the consequences of the sin of others by remaining in "fellowship" with them.

A while ago I attended the annual official meeting of a church I was overseeing. Both the treasurer and the president of the board spoke, and then I addressed the church. I think the message I brought was probably the most severe I have ever given in all my years of church responsibility. I warned the church. I told them about how in Revelation chapter 1 there are seven lampstands representing the seven churches to which Jesus writes the letters (see Rev. 1:20). I went on to point out that in the letter to the church at Ephesus, Jesus tells them that they have lost their first love and how, if they do not repent, He will remove the lampstand from them—it is no longer church (no matter what it calls itself). I gave the church and its leaders time to consider what they wanted to do and, a few months later I removed myself from overseeing them. To this day, they continue in increasing difficulty, although I remain friends with some of the members.

We can read and preach the Bible; but if we fail to be obedient to the voice of God, *what the Spirit is saying to the churches* (see Rev. 2:7,11,17,29; 3:6,13,22), and then we meet in vain. To all seven of the churches in Revelation, the key was not what the Word said, but what the Spirit was saying to that church. Their response to the Spirit was essential. Lack of experience of God, of hearing the voice of the Spirit, is possibly the most dangerous state for any church to be in. The same is true for the individual believer.

While writing this book, it seems to me that there are two things that the Spirit is saying to the church. One is the recognition of the true Body of Christ, regardless of background, history, denomination, or the lack of denomination. The Holy Spirit is bringing a freshness of understanding, mutual respect, and acceptance. Then there is a new sense of breaking fresh ground in our willingness to experience and understand things in Scripture that seem to have been veiled.

For example, there is a new awareness today of angelic presence. As we read Scripture, we are happy to have on record the physical manifestation of angels in both the Old and the New Testaments. There is no reason why we too should not see angels; but some will have to contend for the Truth (what they have experienced) in this.

What will be the result? It's possible to imagine a fresh embracing of Truth by some in various areas of the Church in division. There could be both greater unity and more separation! However, God is a God of revelation. He has revealed Himself to us and He continues to bring to us and others greater understanding and experience. We gain knowledge by the Spirit; it is that kind of knowledge that should increase among God's people. It is important for us to be prepared for unity greater than our current theological stances. We need heart willingness to embrace that, which does not come by natural understanding because it is being revealed by the Spirit.

Church unity in a locality will not come by committee. It will happen as a result of mutual respect and recognition of gift. As I consider the United Kingdom, and other Western nations, it seems to me that there are many cities where international ministries are based but they are not received or recognized by other branches of the Body of Christ within the same city! It is the recognition of those same gifted people that is crucial to becoming unified of the faith (see Eph. 4:11,13). So we need to stay open to the Spirit; He is our Teacher!

Wouldn't it be great if we could all get away from divisive thinking? *I am of Paul* or *I am of Silas*. Won't it be even better if we stop assuming that the numbers of people influenced or the size of church we lead or the number of people we have brought to Christ produces the better "ministry"? The more I examine the New Testament, the more I see *character* as the key ingredient of effective leadership.

Jesus was successful and we should also be a success. However, Jesus was not always *apparently* successful. Difficulties and setbacks can also go with the anointing of God. So, Paul did well. So too did the other disciples who learned from their mistakes and made a difference for the Kingdom of God. Please, can we all do the same?

There is a key mentioned in John chapter 6. Jesus has been giving profound teaching on who He is. Note the passage:

> *It is the Spirit who gives life; the flesh profits nothing; the words that I have spoken to you are spirit and are life. But there are some of you who do not believe. For Jesus knew from the beginning who they were who did not believe, and who it was that would betray Him. And He was saying, "For this reason I have said to you, that no one can come to Me, unless it has been granted him from the Father." As a result of this many of His disciples withdrew, and were not walking with Him anymore. Jesus said therefore to the twelve, "You do not want to go away also, do you?" Simon Peter answered Him, "Lord, to whom shall we go? You have words of eternal life. And we have believed and have come to know that You are the Holy One of God." Jesus answered them, "Did I Myself not choose you, the twelve, and yet one of you is a devil?"* (John 6:63-70).

Jesus is very direct. He tells all His listeners:

❖ You must have the Spirit.

❖ Some of you are unbelievers.

When many stop following Him, He then asks the 12 *"do you want to go away also?"* This provokes the confession of faith in Jesus from Peter. There is no alternative. However, let's consider this from a 21st century perspective. How would people today have viewed Jesus' ministry in the light of these events?

❖ He's lost His significance.

❖ He has too few followers.

❖ He will never regain what He's lost.

Perhaps Paul *was* the most significant of the apostles. Even so, God did not remove from him the *thorn in the flesh* from satan, so as to keep him humble. His experience of the grace of God took him into what may have been considered as:

❖ Unnecessary suffering.

❖ Paul living outside of God's will.

❖ Paul's inability to defeat satan.

❖ A blot on his ministry toward others.

The truth was: God kept him in the understanding that he was what he was by the grace of God and by nothing of his own achievements. We are all in the same grace boat. Perhaps we should note these verses from Romans 12:

> Let love be without hypocrisy. Abhor what is evil; cling to what is good. Be devoted to one another in brotherly love; give preference to one another in honor; not lagging behind in diligence, fervent in spirit, serving the Lord; rejoicing in hope, persevering in tribulation, devoted to prayer, contributing to the needs of the saints, practicing hospitality. Bless those who persecute you bless and curse not. Rejoice with those who rejoice, and weep with those who weep. Be of the same mind toward one another; do not be haughty in mind, but associate with

the lowly. Do not be wise in your own estimation. Never pay back evil for evil to anyone. Respect what is right in the sight of all men. If possible, so far as it depends on you, be at peace with all men.

What's the point? Simply this—Paul learned from his experiences. So too did Jesus (see Heb. 5:8). Paul's relationship with God and its outworking brought him understanding he could never have learned under the gifted teaching of Gamaliel or anyone else for that matter. Experience by the Spirit is our greatest teacher. True theology is the learning of God through experience.

Do not be carried away by varied and strange teachings for it is good for the heart to be strengthened by grace . . . (Hebrews 13:9).

Strange teachings deny the grace of God. Our experience of the Spirit and grace keeps us in the place of right teaching. False doctrine is exhibited through false living. That is why the Scriptures require elders to be people of character, not just ability. Ability or gift not submitted to the grace of God produces arrogance. Our experience of God in grace keeps us on track. It prevents division through selfish ambition. True grace as part of our experience in daily life prevents us from moving into a false doctrine, which allows anyone to do anything. That is why Paul wrote to the Romans:

What shall we say then? Are we to continue in sin that grace might increase? May it never be! How shall we who died to sin still live in it? (Romans 6:1-2).

The key here is about living in it. Living in what? It's a matter of living by choice in the grace experience of God rather than in a sin experience of life.

The Bible tells us that when the church in Jerusalem sent Barnabas to Antioch *he saw the grace of God* (Acts 11:23). The Greek word actually means, "to see." So what did he see? What was it that caused him to go and find Saul (Paul) and take him there? Whatever it was, it ultimately resulted in those two men being released into apostolic ministry by that church.

If grace is to be seen then it is a life experience. It is evident to others. Paul learned grace through experience—just as Jesus did (see Heb. 5:8). When Paul was sent a messenger from satan he sought God about it three times but it was never removed. People looking on could have thought:

- ❖ Paul is backslidden.

- ❖ He can't be in the will of God for this to happen.

- ❖ How can he minister healing to others when he's in that state?

- ❖ God must have abandoned him.

The truth is that God used this attack on Paul's body so Paul could learn from his experience. God's reply to Paul was *my grace is sufficient for you.* (See 2 Cor. 12:7-10.) What was he saying? It was certainly not a rebuke! Paul could continue moving in power to others because as a result of the grace of God toward him he walked in humility. Character was formed to a greater depth through the experience of grace. That is why the grace of God and legalism cannot work together. In church life where both exist, there will never be unity.

Now it is possible to understand the depth of meaning when Paul says *I am what I am by the grace of God.* He did not say *I do what I do.* Grace makes us be what God wants. It is seen when we do what we do from that standpoint of grace.

Conclusion

Truth is a matter of black and white, darkness and light, life and death.

Separation to the Truth means separation from less than the full Truth, not just lies. So in the end, Truth is not a matter of rules but of relationship with the Holy Spirit.

Chapter Sixteen

GENDER ISSUES

This chapter delves into the Truth about gender issues, specifically about women; husbands and wives; and homosexuality. Satan has warped the world's (and unfortunately some churches) perspective about these fundamental issues, and it is having a negative affect on multiple generations.

WOMEN

Women in the Old Testament

One of the most contentious and contended areas of theological and practical dispute is the place of women in the life of the Church of God. Some would say that the church has to move forward from cultural considerations of New Testament times into an acceptance of the full place of women in all church activity. Others hold that there are clear instructions in Scripture that point to a lesser role for women in the life of the church.

This book's crux is that we must trust the Holy Spirit. I would suggest that dogmatic statements do not help us. I have talked with those who say women should have no part in church leadership, and those who say that churches should have women representation in the leadership. This really is where my friend, Ed Paxton, comes in.

Ed and I met in a small restaurant. Our conversation was wide and varied. Eventually we talked about women in church leadership. During our discussion he said, "I'm sure a woman can be an elder." I was shocked. But what shocked me was not the view Ed held (I already knew that). It was the confidence with which he made the comment, and my own awareness of his integrity in making such a statement. At the time I was struggling with the New Testament about the whole area of women leaders. I was convicted in Spirit. I just knew he had to be right to say something as strongly as he did.

I went back into the Scriptures and much of what I write in this chapter comes from the revelation that the Truth comes through the Spirit. What follows is a synopsis of the things God showed me.

The Old Testament spoke of a society under God. It was essentially a male dominated environment. As I looked more closely, I saw less and less legalism from God. Examples of women in the Old Testament follow:

Rahab

Rahab appears in the Book of Joshua. She is a prostitute and a foreigner. There is nothing in the Bible that says she changed her life before or after her encounter with Joshua, except that she protected those of God's people who entered Jericho. Yet she appears in the genealogy of Jesus. Consider:

- ❖ Her lifestyle was inappropriate to become part of the people of God; yet she was received.

- ❖ She was a foreigner, not a Jew, yet she could become a human ancestor of the Messiah.

- ❖ God received her.

- ❖ In the New Testament (Heb. 11:31) Rahab is specifically named as a woman of faith.

Gender Issues

Bathsheba

In many ways Bathsheeba could be seen as a victim. King David spotted her as she was bathing during the night. He sent for and caused her to become pregnant. David did devious things that resulted in the death of Bathsheba's husband. David was the sole guilty party in these things. When the baby was born, it died; David had another child by Bathsheba. His name was Solomon. These are some of the things we can notice from this account:

- ❖ According to the Law both David and Bathsheba should have been killed as a result of their adultery (see Lev. 20:10).

- ❖ The death of the first child could speak of God's judgment.

- ❖ Solomon became King after David.

- ❖ The Messianic line passes from David to Solomon, bringing divine acknowledgment of the union between David and Bathsheba.

- ❖ This account contrasts with David's other wife Michal (the daughter of Saul) who became barren because she despised the King *in her heart* and not because she committed adultery.

- ❖ God's testimony of David was that he was a man after God's own heart (1 Sam. 13:14; Acts 13:22), in spite of all his mistakes.

Deborah

Exceptions break the rule of legalism. Deborah is such a person in Scripture. She was brought up in an essentially male-dominated theocracy and culture, yet she became a powerful ruler of Israel. In the time when Judges ruled Israel, she was one of them. Judges were raised by God to deliver His people from their enemies (Judg. 2:16). In this role, Deborah was powerful and effective. So what can we learn?

- ❖ Even in a male-dominated society like that of the Old Testament, God raised up a woman, even if she was a cultural or even theological exception in her era.

❖ If God chose to raise up a woman in that era, then we should at least allow God to make similar exceptions regarding leadership in the church *even if our literal theology was against that* because we trust the Spirit to lead us.

❖ The real issue is acknowledging what God is saying in order to do it.

Ruth

The story of Ruth is one of the most delightful. She was a foreigner who embraced the Jewish faith and married into it. She became the grandmother of David. As a foreigner she should not have been allowed to marry into the Jewish nation. But God's grace is so great that she, like Rahab, became part of the genealogy of Jesus. This mixed marriage was contrary to Deuteronomy 7:1-4. Ezra led the people in repentance of this same sin in Ezra chapters 9 and 10.

With both Rahab and Ruth, their status was enhanced because they embraced God. Being part of God's people elevated them to a higher place.

Huldah

There are only two parallel references to Huldah in the Old Testament (see 2 Kings 22:14 and 2 Chron. 24:22). Just as her name is the female form of a masculine name, so the title given to her is the female for prophet. In English the word *prophetess* may cause some to demote the person to whom the word is applied, because prophet is considered a higher gift. That is a false assumption. In modern, politically correct parlance we should use the word "prophet" generically. Neither the Hebrew nor the Greek give a distinction other than a linguistic one.

In any case, Huldah clearly pronounces a powerful prophecy bringing clear and direct guidance to the king. He has effectively submitted his kingship to her prophetic authority.

These few examples are sufficient to show that God recognized and used women in authority positions. The fact that there are so few does not mean they should be discounted. Although they seem to be exceptions, that in itself is more than enough to establish their importance under the old covenant. God had people who were not necessarily expected to be used by Him in the spiritual and cultural climate of that time. In the new covenant as we will see, women are given a higher place.

There is just one more interesting matter to mention concerning women in the Old Testament—the phrase: *"Women received back their dead by resurrection"* (Heb. 11:35). Although Rahab is the only woman named in the faith people listed, this phrase speaks of many other women who obtained what they wanted from God *by their own faith* and not that of a male relative.

Women in the New Testament

If we can see such examples in the Old Testament then we should expect to see more women in the New Testament because Jesus came to set people free! In some passages that refer to women and their participation in the life of the church, there is confusion.

In his first letter to the Corinthians, Paul makes two statements:

> *Let the women keep silent in the churches; for they are not permitted to speak, but let them subject themselves, just as the Law also says* (1 Corinthians 14:34).

> *But every woman who has her head uncovered while praying or prophesying, disgraces her head; for she is one and the same with her whose head is shaved* (1 Corinthians 11:5).

At face value, the two contradict. How can a woman pray or prophesy if she is to remain silent? The result of this is that various churches adopt different rulings:

❖ Some say a woman may pray or prophesy but she should have her covered.

❖ Others state that a woman should remain silent and have her head covered.

❖ I have some across others who say a woman should not have her head covered at all, even if she wants to.

❖ Some church groups debate whether a woman may be a priest or not.

There are times when Paul either acts or speaks against his own theology. The circumcision of Timothy is an example. In practice, Paul allowed himself to waiver the letter so he could follow the Spirit. (See Chapter 12.)

So, I believe there are New Testament passages that refer to a specific time or situation. Then there are others that convey principles of fundamental Gospel Truth.

Here is a key passage that illustrates the bigger picture because principles are laid out rather than specific issues being addressed:

> But now that faith has come, we are no longer under a tutor. For you are all sons of God through faith in Christ Jesus. For all of you who were baptized into Christ have clothed yourselves with Christ. There is neither Jew nor Greek, there is neither slave nor free man, there is neither male nor female; for you are all one in Christ Jesus. And if you belong to Christ, then you are Abraham's offspring, heirs according to promise (Galatians 3:24-29).

The *tutor* referred to is the Law (see verse 24), and the word means "a trainer of boys." This is one of the many examples of New Testament passages showing that we are not under the Law, because we have come to faith. The Law makes distinctions. Faith brings equality. That unity is then expressed regardless of racial, social, or gender status.

Oneness is in the status of *Sonship*. This is important because later in the passage Paul speaks of male and female. So Sonship is achieved through faith in Christ. It is open to all. Then verse 28 identifies three categories: Jew and Greek, slave and free man, male and female.

The matter of the Gospel being for Jews and Gentiles (Greeks) was handled during the early church era as recorded in Acts. We have already noted this; particularly how shocked the young church was when the Gentiles experienced the same Spirit of God moving on those divorced from the Jewish faith.

The issue of slave and free could not be handled in the same time period. Paul accepts a cultural climate where slaves are part of everyday life. Today most Christians would agree that slavery does not fit with the Gospel message. Only in the 19th century did people begin to realize how it had no place in the Kingdom of God. William Wilberforce was a prime mover in bringing about the abolition of slavery in England. Now it is an accepted fact that slavery is wrong.

It is only in more recent times that there has been any shift in the status of women. Galatians 3:25 should have prepared God's people for the transition that would come. It is now here. I believe it is part of the ushering in of the end of the times of the Gentiles. It is part of the end-times process. However, just as Jewish believers were shocked when the Gentiles received the Spirit, so we too can fail to see what is already established in Scripture.

I appreciate that what I have written will be contentious to some. My question would be *why?* Surely we should be able to stop and reconsider things in the light of further revelation, much as the apostles did as recorded in Acts. If we hold an entrenched view, then we are really saying we are not open to the Holy Spirit—the source of Truth. In any case, it should not be necessary to set things in a legalistic format, as we have confidence in the Spirit.

This is the real issue. The only reason we now have so many dogmatic statements of faith practice is because for centuries the church lost its sense of the leading of God's Spirit. If the church can come to an understanding and fresh embracing of the Holy Spirit for the decisions that are to be made, then we will have a different, better church because she decides on the basis of *what seems good to us and the Holy Spirit.*

With specific regard to women and their place in the work of God, it is the Spirit who should decide. We cannot raise a voice against that which God, by the Spirit, honors. We must continue in the vein of what the Spirit says to the church(es). Jezebel was not held in question because she was a woman who claimed to have gift. The real problem was her lack of godly character revealed in her immorality (see Rev. 2:18-21).

Since we have the Holy Spirit, there is no need to decide in advance whether:

- ❖ A woman can have a ministry.

- ❖ She can be in church leadership.

- ❖ She can speak in a meeting or not.

- ❖ She should have her head covered.

If the Spirit tells us, then we do it without consideration to doctrinal practice or tradition. We trust His leading. We do not deny how the Spirit is using women in the church today. How dare we, if He honors those women with gift and anointing?

Husband and Wife

It must be at least 20 years ago when a married couple came to Christ and joined the church I was then leading. Let's call them Alf and Jennie. They had two happy children and the family was consistent in their attendance.

One Sunday morning, Alf appeared at the service with the children but Jennie was not with them. When I asked him if she was alright, he told me he didn't know where she was. Later that day I received a phone call from a woman in the church. She informed me that Jennie was at her house. I asked if she would see me. Jennie turned up some time later.

I walked into the room of our house where Jennie was sitting. She glared at me angrily and said, "You'll never get me to go back to him, never"! I replied, "No, I don't think I will. Whatever has he done"?

Jennie's jaw dropped. She had convinced herself that I would take a legalistic approach with her, that I would quote Bible verses and force her to return home. Instead we talked for about half an hour. Then I asked her if she would wait while I went to see Alf. She agreed.

I talked with Alf. He was defensive. He told me she was not in submission to him and she should return home. I asked him what gave him the right to demand that. He told me the Scriptures were clear on what Jennie should do. I agreed. I then asked him if he was clear on what the Scriptures might have to say to him as a husband. We then talked about the husband loving the wife as Christ loved the Church and gave Himself for her. An interesting discussion ensued:

"Will you tell her to come back, Tony?"

"No," I replied.

"Will you ask her to come back?"

"I might," I replied.

"Will you say please?" Alf said.

"Yes," I replied, "I'll do that."

Please remember this goes back years. I was definitely in my infancy concerning moving sharply in the Spirit. I remain a learner today. However, when I returned to my house, my ensuing conversation with Jennie astonished me:

"I've see Alf," I said. "He asks will you please return home."

Jennie's reply shocked me. "Did he say *please?*" she asked.

"As a matter of fact, he did."

"I'm going back," she said.

To this day they have not separated since. That experience taught me so much.

There is too much focus on women in submission but actually love comes into the marriage situation through the husband. Submission is a response to love, not a legal requirement. Just as Jesus has love for the church, so the husband is to love the wife.

Some years ago Margaret and I were taught that the husband, as the head of the home, should manage the household finances and accounts. We tried to do it that way but it was a disaster. Not because I was useless but because Marg was better than me at it. What we had been taught (and told to practice!) dishonored Marg's abilities.

Some years ago a woman came back to God. She was living with her boyfriend and they had children. She started attending meetings and made a reservation to attend our annual church holiday. Her boyfriend decided he would come too but would not attend the meetings. He was definitely not a Christian.

By the end of the week he was born again. Soon after that, one of our leaders suggested to me that the boyfriend should move out. I replied, "No. I think we need to stop trying to do the Holy Spirit's work for Him." Weeks later, the couple decided to marry. It was a great celebration. He testified during the ceremony. The Holy Spirit had done His work!

Homosexuality

When we look at the matter of homosexuality, we see a different arena of Truth. There is nowhere in the Scriptures that would allow for such a practice. Both the Old and New Testaments are consistent in this matter:

> *God gave them over to degrading passions; for their women exchanged the natural function for that which is unnatural, and in the same way also the men abandoned the natural function of the woman and burned in their desire toward one another, men with men committing indecent acts and receiving in their own persons the due penalty of their error* (Romans 1:26-27).

Although God disapproves of the activity, He still loves all people. Some time ago a young man entered one of our services and I knew him to be a practicing homosexual. At the end of the service, I went straight to him and hugged him. He just sobbed in my arms. He knew I disapproved of what he did; he now knew that I still had love for him.

All sin is sin! When we move toward others in the Spirit then the love of God flows to them through us.

So what do we say? God always loves the person even if He does not like the practice. Any practicing homosexual needs to know from us as God's people that He loves that person. Any change in life should start at the Cross, the place of repentance. It will be necessary to discuss a change in lifestyle with the person: but any such change is part of their repentance toward God because they love Him, not because we present a Gospel of legalism.

Conclusion

Whenever difficult situations arise, trust the Spirit. Every believer has had moments when we didn't know what to do. Worrying never helps! Trust the Spirit of Truth—let Him lead and guide you.

Books to help you grow strong in Jesus

Additional copies of this book and
other book titles from
DESTINY IMAGE EUROPE
are available at your local bookstore.

We are adding new titles every month!

To view our complete catalog on-line, visit us at:

www.eurodestinyimage.com

Send a request for a catalog to:

Via Acquacorrente, 6
65123 - Pescara - ITALY
Tel. +39 085 4716623 - Fax +39 085 4716622

* *

Are you an author?

Do you have a "today" God-given message?

CONTACT US

We will be happy to review your
manuscript for a possible publishing:

publisher@eurodestinyimage.com